THE WORLD & I IN 2015

Control Your Destiny

By
Max Liang Choon Chuan
&
Lee McKing

All enquiries, including enquiries seeking permission, should be addressed to:
INSIGHTS LIFE MENTOR
140 Paya Lebar Road, AZ@Paya Lebar, #08-17, Singapore 409015
Main line: 6748 6279
Website: www.yishu.com.sg

If you would like to have your views on the subject reviewed and/or published, please contact us at www.yishu.com.sg.

ISBN 978-981-09-3299-2

Published by Liang Choon Chuan, 2014

Contents

Foreword

Some people seem to attract wealth, power, luck and success without much effort while some people have to put in a great deal of effort to achieve the same results. Others, however, don't succeed at all and fail miserably in their endeavours. Why is this so and what happens to each of them?

On numerous occasions, we have heard that the successful seems to know what is happening in the future that enable them to make the right choices at the most opportune time. That I agree without doubt, they do have the kind of networks and contacts that is able to give them the insights into the running of the ground situations and economies; which allows them to make the right decision at the right time as if they have the "gift" of seeing into the future. Wouldn't you be keen to know the future too and make informed choices in your actions to fully take advantage of the situation?

Wouldn't you take the opportunity of knowing what could happen in the near future to take necessary precautions against a market heading south or when the market is moving up? How about being in the right market segment at the right time to take advantage of the peaks and troughs of market cycle?

How about having the information on hand to help you decide on the business direction as well as whether to take a defensive stance or an all-out offensive. Would such information be useful to you in your everyday life or business?

Foreword

We tell you what is going to happen in the world this coming 2015 for you to take full advantage of it, be it good or bad.

I am pretty sure that all of you would also like to know what would be in store for you personally in the days and months to come. Would you meet someone special, run a risk of marriage issue or opportunities in work and career? You may also like to know if it is a year for you to take a step back or to work your heart out to achieve what you want to achieve.

Various astrologers have tried in various ways to predict what will happen in the near future but none have been written in such details and backed by Science to give much credence to the information presented.

"The world and I in 2015" will tell you all that you want to know in the most comprehensive manner, giving you insights into every single occurrence that may happen to you and in the world. This will be a book to give you the timeline to prepare for the future that is unfolding and to take the actions required.

Everyone that holds the information in "The world and I in 2015" will be the masters of opportunities so limitless that it will be most bewildering to others. They will hold an inconceivable advantage over the multitude of people.

About Yishu Insights

Yishu Insights is helmed by Max Liang and specializes in the area of Modern Energy Geomancy (Feng Shui), Physiognomy (Mian Xiang), I-Ching and Numerology. Yishu Insights was developed from the need to create a platform for the development and research into the science of Nature as well as to provide quality coursework and services in various areas, such as Geomancy (Feng Shui) Audits, Life Path Consultation and Physiognomy Reading. Currently, all techniques are incorporated into Success Coaching where business owners and corporate executives get specialized coaching to achieve results towards a more rounded success in their career, business, personal development, family and more!

The name Yishu（易数）is derived from the Chinese I-Ching（易经）and Numbers（数字）. Thus, Yishu represents the combined methodology from the East and West that has been fine-tuned into a system that we employ. We are able to effectively decipher and gain greater insights into our own lives and in effect provide essential, targeted directions and actions to propel one's life to the next level of success.

About the authors

Max Liang is a scientist and possesses a BSc. (Hons) degree in Life Sciences. As he was trained in the pure sciences, he does not believe in the field of metaphysics. However, circumstance requires that he equip himself with a tool to tell a person's character from their physical attributes thereby leading him to body language and face reading. He subsequently embarked on the study of Physiognomy (面相), a method developed through generations to compare facial and physical attributes to human character; to learn the skill and apply in everyday life.

His interest in the Chinese Metaphysics was piqued by the constant discovery of applicable knowledge and through the past nine years, he studied further under various masters in I-Ching (易经) Bazi （八字）, Fengshui （风水）, Numerology and Advanced Physiognomy and attained the level of Advanced Life Destiny Forecaster (高级预测师) under China ZhouYi Association (中华周易协会) (CZY).

Max provides Fengshui audits, both for home owners and corporate clients and also conducts Numerology and Face Reading courses. Currently, he delivers Life Mentor programs and Success Coaching for individuals and also acts as adviser to small and medium enterprises (SME); assisting them to improve their business by applying the methodology that we developed.

About the authors

Lee McKing has a Dip. In Child Psychology & Early Education and got pulled into the world of numerology by accident.

Discovering that he had a talent with numbers in 2012, he started off by using numerology to entertain and astound his friends. However, after accurately diagnosing his grandfather's colon and prostate cancer, he realized the potential of how he can help people using this profiling tool.

McKing also picked up the basics of Neuro-Linguistic Programming and its mastery level in 2014 and realized that both tools can be used to help people more effectively.

McKing currently does numerology consultations for people for clarity about their life and potential and provide NLP sessions for people who desire change for themselves.

THE WORLD IN 2015

What is the affecting element in 2015?

The world is running on the Wood Goat Year based on Chinese metaphysics in the Year 2015. The combined element of Wood and Earth element of the goat presents a Wood Earth Clash and also diminishes the effect of water and creates a drying effect. In numerology terms we are running an 8 Year which translates to a strong fire element. Intrinsically, we face a very weak Water element.

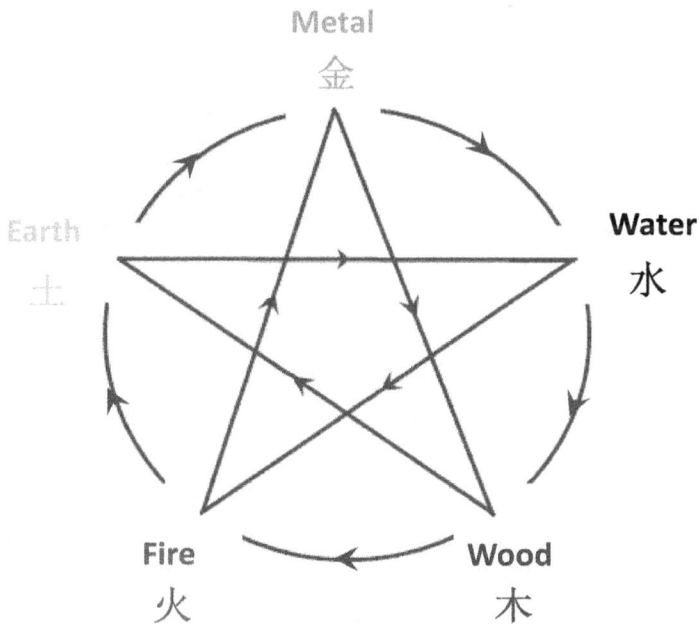

Outlook of the world in 2015

This year, squabbling and arguments between countries will continue. There is a chance that countries may face a lot of obstacles in their communication leading to provocation. Countries may also be stressed financially making everyone very busy and stressed. There will be a lot of movement around the world for monetary gains.

In 2015, as we see a Wood Earth Clash, we might see an increase in Earth movement and volcanic activity. Wood Earth clash also represents sickness and death and may entail massive loss of lives. The combined effect of Fire element into the equation actually reduces the effect of Wood element and drive up Earth element, this generally denotes a case of increasing bacterial disease and makes the possibility of Earth movement more pronounced. There will be a lot of fire issues, possibly serious forest fire and drought will be a common occurrence. War may break out with a lot of political instability in various countries. There may be a possibility of mass death in the natural environment.

Industries affected adversely are mostly water, metal and fire related. Throughout the world there will be a lot of stress on the shipping and logistics sector, commodities may be affected as well. Most of the service sector will also be affected except for those supporting movement of people. The electronics, software, internet, petrochemical sector will be adversely affected as well. Finally the Financial sector will face a slowdown and lead to another reorganization and consolidation.

YEAR 2015 & YOU

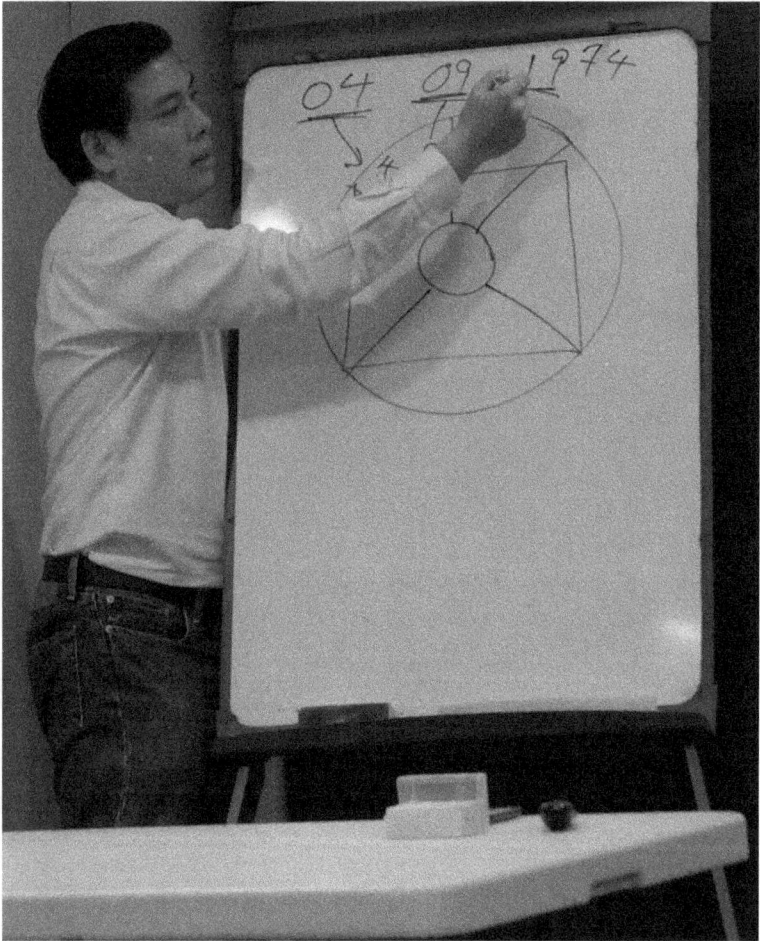

Year 2015 & YOU!

We find ourselves believing that each new year will bring better luck or fortune, but how can we determine whether it truly is a good year or not?

Many people look to the zodiac or the stars for some sign, especially when the New Year is starting, and hope for some good indications for that year.

Here at Yishu Insights, we use numerology as our basis to discover whether it is truly a good year for us or not... and this book teaches you how to find your yearly outlook for 2015!

Firstly, we must add up our day and month and reduce the numbers to a single digit by adding.

Example 1:   01 Feb is 01/02, and adding them up we get 3

Example 2:   12 Apr is 12/04, and adding up we get 16, which we reduce to a single digit by adding them up again, so 1 + 6 = 7

Example 3:   29 Oct is 29/10, and adding up we get 39, which we reduce to a single digit by adding them up again, so 3 + 9 = 12, and once more, 1 + 2 = 3

So what is your number? Once you get this number, flip to the relevant page to find out your yearly outlook for 2015!!

Year 2015 & YOU!

What is the number you found? Below, you will find the relevant page to go to, once you identified your number.

Within each number chapter, there are also individual years to refer to when you are looking up what the Year 2015 means to you!

If the number you found was the number 1:

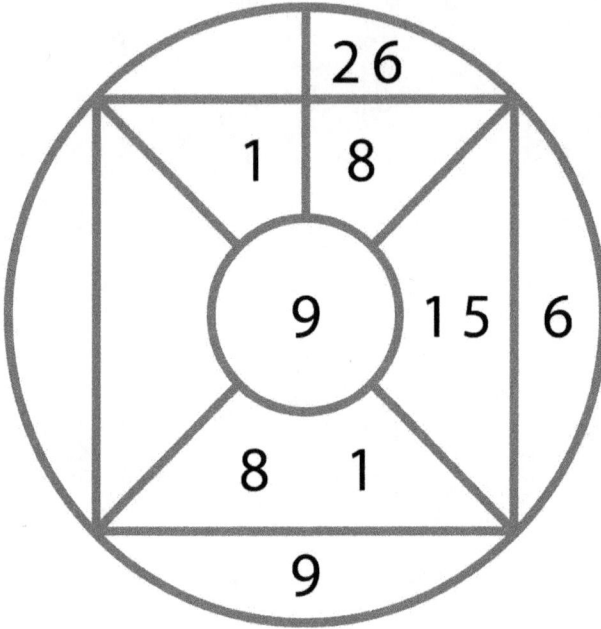

The initial few months of 2015, you may engage in certain independent tasks that may not feel right to you. In whatever you do, you may feel incredibly stressed to do all by yourself. In fact, do be aware that there may be legal implications for you this year. You may find yourself doing things by yourself starting a project alone and finishing off alone as well. This year you may also be busy looking for job opportunities. Even though you are so stressed and busy, as long as you can persevere and pull through, you will see what you desired. Therefore, your hard work will pay off this year and see you great success.

For people born in 1901, 1910, 1919, 1928, 1937, 1946, 1955, 1964, 1973, 1982 and 1991, you really have to be aware of what you want to do because otherwise, you end up creating your own obstacles. In fact, what you did just at the end of last year may have already created some issues with your friends. Technically, you already know what you want to do, but you keep thinking about it and seeking ways to not do it. You may find that you already spend your life going around in circles, it is up to you to decide and act on your decision in order to succeed in life and make it happen. This is the year where you can achieve success, but only if you are decisive and take action. You will also find that you suddenly have an expanding network and while this is good, it has its own setback in that some people may try to use you, so take heed and be aware. For some of you, you will find that you have to do presentations in order to make it, and planning and scheduling all the items suddenly seems daunting. There will be a lot of communication about the changes to take place and you may find yourself temperamental and angry, however, if you use those feelings to motivate you towards your goals, you will definitely be able to make it this year. Those anger issues can also be putting more strain on your heart, so please be aware especially if you are so angry all the time. Marriage issues may prevail so work life balance and good communication is key this year. Ulitmately, you can achieve success this year through good communication, work life balance, and working towards what you want!

For children born in 2009, they may find themselves more emotional this year. Temper tantrums are more likely and communication may get to be quite heated. What these children do not yet realize, is that they are limiting their own development by being so emotional and resistant to guidance. Once they are able to calm their nerves and do what they are told, they will see their own achievements easily.

For people born in 1902, 1911, 1920, 1929, 1938, 1947, 1956, 1965, 1974, 1983 and 1992, the success you saw last year is being replicated this year, congratulations! Although this year brings some stress and frustration especially when it involves communication, it is all worth it when your hard work pays off in the end. Continue to seek your means to success and be creative and motivated. Your key to success is by ensuring that your plans and course of action is in sync. You are meticulous and usually plan in great detail, however, if you have not achieved your success yet, it may be that you are too indecisive and delay too much by "over" planning your process. Remember that all planning and no action equals nothing get done! Another thing to note is to be aware of what you say, not to be too direct and straightfroward as that may either cause issues for you or hurt others unintentionally. So speak at the right time with the right people to get your desired results to take place! There may be career opportunities overseas and should you recognize it to be necessary for your success, take it! Similar to last year, once you have thought out the process, you need to communicate to the right people for them to take action with you. Continue with your plans and knowing the right actions to take, and truly, no one can stop you in achieving results this year!

For children born in 2001 and 2010, parents need to take note that all their learning efforts will come to fruition this year, if they persevered with what they started last year. If they have mentors or study partners, it may propel them in achieving great success this year. Do note that they will be more vocal in what they want to achieve this year. Just remind them that their rewards commensurate with their effort and that enduring through the stress will see great success and achievements this year!

For people born in 1903, 1912, 1921, 1930, 1939, 1948, 1957, 1966, 1975, 1984 and 1993, beware of ups and downs in your business and career this year. What you had planned in 2014 may get stolen by some people making you very angry and these saboteurs are still evident this year as well. You also have to take note of your plans and actions and ensure that they are aligned, so that you do not veer off track. Now, be very careful not to take actions until you have a good concrete plan. Any impulsive actions with no plan to fall back on may cause more harm than good. Also, be careful of a possible heart condition that causes a health issue. Fortunately, you will have the opportunities to give advice to others and may attract a lot of supporters to you, so do take those opportunities to increase your network. Overall this year, you may experience higher expenditure and may be made to spend large amount of money, this may be the cause of your business failure. Of course, you are a brave soul and do not fear the hard knocks in life, however, do take heed from a little advice in this book.

For children born in 2002 and 2011, there is some indication of family issues within the family that may affect the child internally. These children may be a bit stubborn to seek out people such as friends or teachers in order to find someone who can be there for them and keep their issues in their heart. Others may seek out the wrong people instead, hence, they need to be aware that some of the people they seek may bring them bad influence. Although this year seems to be good for studies, when these children can shift their focus into academies, they have to be aware of their emotional needs as well.

For people born in 1904, 1913, 1922, 1931, 1940, 1949, 1958, 1967, 1976, 1985 and 1994, did you take up the opportunity to go over-seas for career prospects just recently? You may notice that there are such opportunities appearing again this year. However, at the same time, don't be too rash and just go for all overseas trips, you need to plan and prioritise which trips are of greater value. This will allow you to use the least effort to amass the greatest pros-pects. Because of the high returns you enjoy this year, you may attract saboteurs who incidentally may be the same people from last year! Another thing to note is to stick to your principles and follow a set of morals and you will always go the right path. This is crucial because this year you will have a lot of opportunities to meet people of high net worth. Going the right path for your-self, means that you will not be too greedy and will gain much more from it. Also, this year presents an interesting opportunity for yourself, of either mentoring a person of high potential or to find a mentor for yourself. And although it is true that no one can stop you from amassing such high returns, you might want to take note of two things. Firstly, the best path may not always be smooth, and secondly, the higher you rise, the greater chance you can fall. For the older folks, please remember to take care of your health!

For children born in 2003 and 2012, there is some indication of family issues that may affect them emotionally. These children may shut off totally from what is going on around them. If you know of such children, do look out for them. These children tend to bottle up their feelings and emotions and may suffer from a deeper hurt. They are not likely to seek help openly and may not realise that they need help. These children may seem to be doing well academically, so you may not be able to read their emotional turmoil, you may need to be more aware of their social and emo-tional development.

For people born in 1900, 1905, 1914, 1923, 1932, 1941, 1950, 1959, 1968, 1977, 1986 and 1995, similar to last year, this year may also have career opportunities overseas. You may find yourself a bit hard on cash at the moment and yet have to spend money on other people. Some of you will be reluctant to do so, thus, making for an interesting yet stressful thinking process. For the older folk, you may meet someone who you can mentor into a greater individual, and for the younger ones, you may meet your own mentor. Do be careful of your heart as there is some health risk here. However, if you are looking for a relationship, do keep your eyes peeled as someone may appear in your life this year! You have opprotunities to increase your network and it may be among this kind of network in which you can find that potential partner, whether for career or for relationship. Do note that there is a higher chance for aggressive speech leading to stress and tension in your relationships with people, so be aware of what you say and how you say it. If you are able to use this energy to motivate people when you speak, you are able to move people and shift mountains. It may be a good idea to know the strengths and weaknesses of the people around you in order for you to motivate them further. in fact, knowing their characteristics will help propel you further whether its it for career or relationships and friendships.

For those children born in 2004 and 2013, there may be opportunities to travel and move about be it changing school or moving house. Don't keep your emotions to yourself as such changes are not easy. It is definitely a time for exploration and meeting new friends. For the children born in 2004, just be aware that the person you meet may just be a crush so don't fall too deeply! These children may be more daring and willing to take risks, so do watch out for them especially if it is physical risk!

For people born in 1906, 1915, 1924, 1933, 1942, 1951, 1960, 1969, 1978, 1987 and 1996, this year is an emotional year for you. There will be cases of anger, stress and frustration. Do take precaution for we see evidence of a heart issue arising. You start off with getting some extra cash but you have to be careful of your expenditure. You are a sociable person but this year, you may spend too much on your friends and network, although some of you might think that it is a good investment as these network can bring you more business. The latter half of 2015 sees you busy with planning and quite stressed too. There is a hint of marriage or relationship issues as well, and it is all because of your focus in your career and business. Hence, overall, some investments might be good but you need to take calculated risks. Also, remember that family and relationships are equally important so do divide your time wisely.

For children born in 2000, 2005 and 2014, especially for the 9 and 14 year olds, these children may find that they need to focus on presentations in school this year. These presentations may give them stress but they just need to know that everyone is going through it and to believe in themselves. They may also face peer pressure that seems to be worse this year as compared to last year, and they need to stand strong with their sense of responsibility and not give in. There is also a chance for family issues but once again, they need to stand strong and firm. However, someone needs to be there to affirm the baby that everything will be alright.

For people born in 1907, 1916, 1925, 1934, 1943, 1952, 1961, 1970, 1979, 1988 and 1997, this year you need to show your worth and you will have people who can aid you! It is a great year for networking and perhaps a benefactor or mentor might appear to guide you as well. This is a busy and stressful year where you might be searching for opportunities in career or investments. An interesting thing is that investments may yield great rewards for you this year! But do be careful of possible legal matters that arise from your dealing with people though. This is an excellent year for you to take action with your plans and seek the right people for your own success. Just remember to say the right thing, at the right time, and take calculated risks when possible!

For the children born in 2006, they are one busy bunch. They may meet someone who can guide them this year. This is a stressful year for them, and they really need that guidance, especially in dealing with stress and their emotions. Some of these children may blurt accidentally under emotional stress and hurt others' feelings or say the wrong things at the wrong time. So be there for them to tide them over the issues they may face. This is a time for them to make new friends but be aware of who they mix with as they may come across some bad influence.

For people born in 1908, 1917, 1926, 1935, 1944, 1953, 1962, 1971, 1980, 1989 and 1998, this year is a stressful and busy year for you. You have to be careful of possible legal matters, although that is probably one of the reasons this year is so stressful for you. There are also issues that cause anger and frustration, as well as relationship and marriage issues. You will be busy looking for business opportunities. Your career and business may give you problems that you end up feeling frustrated and stressed. You may also be stressed out from being tasked to conduct presentations. Be mindful of the words you say, as you may unintentionally offend someone this year. To sum up, this year's advice is that you need to endure through the stress and frustration and you can make it!

For children born in 2007, these children need to be strong as there are some indications of family issues within the family that may cause unnecessary stress and tension on them. They may be forced to be in a situation where they are separated from their family. The frustration will lead them onto an emotional path, some throwing temper tantrums in school, while others may keep the hurt within themselves. Therefore, they need people to be with them and help them tide through the turmoil that may come. Chances are, Year 2015 will be a busy year for them.

For people born in 1909, 1918, 1927, 1936, 1945, 1954, 1963, 1972, 1981, 1990 and 1999, this year sees some expenditure for you. The expenditure that goes into investments might be a good idea if you take some calculated risks. Money goes in and out easily this year so make sure it goes into well thought out investments that give great returns! There may be some instability in your business or career so do be prepared for what may happen. You also have to do some independent tasks which can be done rather half-heartedly because you keep thinking about the options and procrastinate. Honestly, you need to be more decisive and move on! Even though you may find that you have to do things by yourself like a one-man-show, the actions you take ultimately determines your success! Year 2015 is a year that is full of opportunities to achieve success and wealth, so best seize it and act to make it a dream come true!

For children born in 2008, this year sees these children being more independent. Although they are unsure and wary, it will be a good opportunity for them to learn to be independent. You may find that these children start to keep things to themselves especially with them being emotional children, just keep you're an eye on them and ensure that they are doing right.

If the number you found was the number 2:

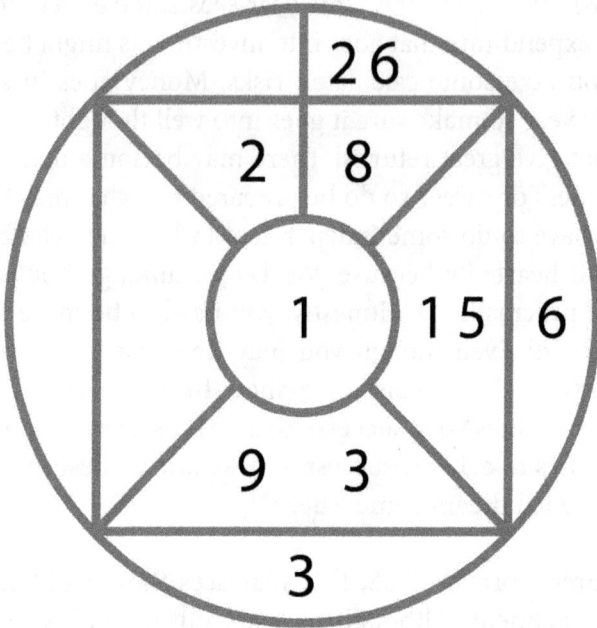

The initial few months deals a lot with communication especially with the network you build up last year. This year, you will encounter the pressure of communication with others. You will get busy fast as time goes and early in the year you may encounter signs of legal matters that you have to go through. Generally, as long as you are unable to communicate to people what you want exactly, you will end up doing things by yourself, like a one-man-show. Your business or career will be very fast moving as well, especially for short term businesses. Just be aware of possible fast and aggressive expenditures near to the end of the year.

For people born in 1901, 1910, 1919, 1928, 1937, 1946, 1955, 1964, 1973, 1982 and 1991, you need to take caution with the words you say, as you may unintentionally hurt others' feelings when you are too straightforward. Especially with the network you build up last year. Otherwise, you may face difficulty with people and supporters. This year is all about the actions you need to take, there is no point just saying and not doing. When this happens, you will find that your plans will come to fruition and no one can stop you from achieving your success. However, do be wary that too much focus in your career and business may lead to problems with relationships and family. Hence, finding the balance between work and play is truly important this year, and hopefully, that is the success you are striving for as well.

Now for children born in 2009, they may be very blunt with their words and find themselves saying the wrong thing at the wrong time. There is also some anger issues which may lead to problems with their friends. These children need a mentor to guide them in planning and taking action, in their studies as well as their co-curricular activities. Doing so will allow them to achieve success.

For people born in 1902, 1911, 1920, 1929, 1938, 1947, 1956, 1965, 1974, 1983 and 1992, the initial few months of 2015 sees a lot of communication but no action that is being taken. It appears that you are indecisive about something. Perhaps you are afraid of taking action with all the stress and frustration that you might already be facing or fear to face. However, do you know that talking and planning but not taking action will be a huge waste to your time and efforts? If you are not careful, there is a huge expenditure this year and you may face losses. There appears to be opportunities to go overseas for work related matters. Therefore, do be more decisive and take the necessary action for your success.

For children born in 2001 and 2010, this year sees a lot of communication involved. Some of the children may even be spending too much time talking and planning. They crux of the matter is that they need to take action. Do be mindful that they may have a crush this year, or even get into a relationship. Some may try to take some risks which may result in injury, so do be aware. Some risk taken will also result in huge financial losses.

For people born in 1903, 1912, 1921, 1930, 1939, 1948, 1957, 1966, 1975, 1984 and 1993, this year is full of challenges for you but you can see the silver lining as you persevere. There may be instability in your work or career and you may experience a lot of fast-paced work. As you are busy this year, your health may be affected, especially the heart and circulatory system. You have to be careful not to be too rash otherwise for it may lead to financial losses. Problems and obstacles will appear by the middle of the year, and this further creates stress and frustration for you. You may become frustrated and stressed when dealing with people and you might need to delegate your task to others. Bear with the stress and pressure from the people around you for there may be financial rewards in the end. There is chance for communication breakdown here, so do explain what you want and need clearly.

For children born in 2002 and 2011, this year sees some family issues for them that will cause stress and tension. This is a challenging year for them to go through. The children born in 2002 might seek comfort elsewhere, such as with friends or with someone else. The family needs to learn how to manage their affairs in an orderly manner. Their communication may become more aggressive and may cause more challenges for them. However, this year is a year where they will meet new people and foster new friendship.

For people born in 1904, 1913, 1922, 1931, 1940, 1949, 1958, 1967, 1976, 1985 and 1994, this year brings in money but also stress and saboteurs. As you plan by yourself without others knowing and being too hasty in your plans, your plan may lack detail thereby attracting saboteurs who sees that you did not think to completion and may want to use that to their advantage. Hence, it might be a good idea to slow down and plan through more thoroughly. You may do some presentations to earn your money and may lead you to be busy. You may even need to rush through your presentation. You may find that the more you plan your budget, the more stressed out you become. It might be time for you to seek advice from experts. You might be in the position this year to provide advice to others and you sure look for success in what you do. Finally, do be wary as there may be legal matters for you this year.

For children born in 2003 and 2012, they may face some family issues this year. They may be very obsessed with planning what they want to do or even their future. However, these children may be more secretive and may not want to tell anyone what is happening at home. Hence, people around them to be more aware of these children and how they feel, especially when this is a stressful year for them. They may also be in need of money due to some plans that they make and this may make them to be very busy.

For people born in 1900, 1905, 1914, 1923, 1932, 1941, 1950, 1959, 1968, 1977, 1986 and 1995, this year is a great year for you to build up your network, and you might even meet a rich and influential person to be your mentor. However, you have to watch what you say, as you can be quite aggressive when you speak this year, which may hurt people without you knowing, especially when you speak too fast. There is also a chance for a relationship partner this year, just be wary to split your time and resources evenly. This is because you may have ups and downs in your business or career, so do be aware. Engaging is contract based business may be good this year. Learn to delegate your task out this year and manage the stress that others exert on you, financial gains may be in sight.

For those children born in 2004 and 2013, this year brings many opportunities for them to make new friends! For those born in 2004, they may have a crush on someone, however, they have to be aware to spend more time on their studies. These children can be prone to explosive bursts of words this year, especially when they are under stress, so guidance must be there to teach them how to manage stress and anger. This year will be a year of massive results for them if they are able to plan sufficiently and be motivated to achieve their results with a purpose in mind.

For people born in 1906, 1915, 1924, 1933, 1942, 1951, 1960, 1969, 1978, 1987 and 1996, this year is a stressful year especially when it involves money. You may experience high expenditure going into many areas such as for investments, medical, expenses, property, legal matters etc. This may create financial stress on you. You should also be careful as there may be backstabbers in your career or business. This is truly a busy year with you needing to solve issues from seemingly everywhere. One good thing is that there might be an opportunity for you to travel overseas but just plan for unexpected situations that may occur while you are away from work. This year is a good year for investment and if you can take some calculated risk in this area, return can be rather good. If you are in business, opportunities are abound for you to take.

For children born in 2000, 2005 and 2014, this year is a stressful year for them. They may face family issues that give them emotional stress. They may start to have a strong perception towards money and may talk about money more frequently. Planning and talking about money and trying to be make some money for themselves will probably make them very busy, but it may be a case of "busy for nothing". These children may also need to move around this year be it house or school, or even overseas travel for them.

For people born in 1907, 1916, 1925, 1934, 1943, 1952, 1961, 1970, 1979, 1988 and 1997, once you do what you say, and prove that you have that potential, you are bound to have people willing to help you! This year is a great year for you, with lots of networking and maybe even benefactors or mentors coming to help you in your business. With so much networking this year, you may even meet someone of personal interest, which is good for the singles, but not as much for the taken (so take heed). Of course, just be aware that with so much good, you might attract a backstabber or two. This is also an excellent year for you to take action with your plans and gather all the people you need for your own success. Just remember, you probably need to talk in order to build your network that much faster so say the right thing, at the right time!

For the children born in 2006, they will meet and make a lot of friends this year. However, they have to be more careful with their words because they might unintentionally hurt others' when they speak. Some of these children are very blunt and straightforward, while others seem to say the wrong things at the wrong time. Regardless of the situation, remind them to be careful with their words and be mindful of others' situation before speaking.

For people born in 1908, 1917, 1926, 1935, 1944, 1953, 1962, 1971, 1980, 1989 and 1998, this year is a really stressful year filled with anger issues, frustration and tension. The year begins with communication stress, which may result in anger especially when there is a chance of legal matters that you need to settle this year as well. There is also a sign of marriage or relationship issues. However, amidst all the problems and issues, this year can become a successful year for you! You may have to do tasks by yourself, like a one-man-show, and it may be very fast, short term or contract-based, but it will be successful. Think before you talk, and do what you say, and most things will fall into place.

For children born in 2007, there may be family issues arising at home, such as arguments and quarrels. This results in ever-changing emotions of anger, stress and frustration. The people around these children need to realize what is going on, although it may be quite obvious from all the anger and frustration from the children. More importantly, help and guidance must be provided to them to help them cope, or if you are the parents, solve your issues quietly and orderly!

For people born in 1909, 1918, 1927, 1936, 1945, 1954, 1963, 1972, 1981, 1990 and 1999, this year is all about communication and talking a lot about business and career. Although for some of you, you might be talking more about the investment profits that you are making this year. For those who have not invested, do calculated risk management and get a good expert if possible to assist with the investments. This year sees quite a few presentations that need to be made in order for you to earn money. Plan them well and conduct them artfully!

For children born in 2008, as they are children who do not talk much or say what they are truly thinking, these children will be more secretive this year. It is that age of independent thinking. They will also pick up skills such as show-and-tell, in order to learn how to present themselves and an item as preparation for the next phase of academics. You may also find them to be talking about different jobs that they want to do this year!

If the number you found was the number 3:

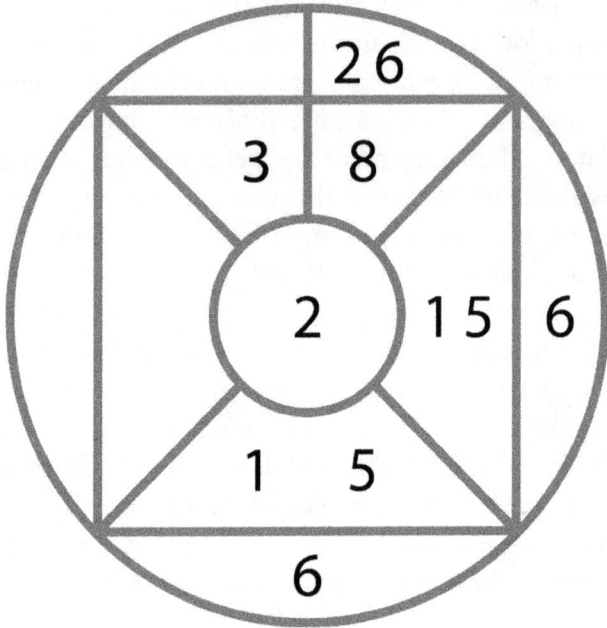

Stress and frustration from the previous year may have carried over into 2015 especially the first few months of the year. The stress and frustration show in your communication and you may unintentionally hurt others when speaking especially when you are too blunt and straightforward. Basically, manage your stress well, and maintain your relationships with your friends. There is also an opportunity for you to travel overseas because of work and make more money due to your venture, you may also be able to curb your spending and see some savings in the end. Overall, this year seems to be another busy year for you.

For people born in 1901, 1910, 1919, 1928, 1937, 1946, 1955, 1964, 1973, 1982 and 1991, you may face more emotional issues this year. Perhaps it is because of the stress and tension from work, but you have to control your anger. Being angry does not help anything, and worsens your relationship with your friends and family. Hence, do be careful of potential marriage and family issues. In your haste, you may grab any network opportunities that come by but you should still be wary of their true intentions. However, do consider such networking to meet a benefactor or mentor that can guide you in developing yourself further. With that guidance, you can think and plan what you want and be able to achieve success more easily. We can never emphasize the importance of planning sufficiently and this year is a year of planning for you to find way, regardless of how stressful the planning can get.

For children born in 2009, these children may face a number of anger and emotional issues this year. They need to learn how to slow down and not be so rash. Taking the time to study the necessary details will help them in their academic front. They will meet a mentor or two this year, but this may not necessarily mean a tuition teacher! They can be quite hard-headed though, so it really depends on whether they like the teacher or not! There is a chance that they are keen in certain purchases and they don't mind finding the money themselves, this may cause them to move around and meet more people.

For people born in 1902, 1911, 1920, 1929, 1938, 1947, 1956, 1965, 1974, 1983 and 1992, you will have more challenges this year that can create additional stress and tension leading you to be in a more emotional state. The great thing is that once you are able to overcome these challenges, you will see great success! Being stressed and emotional, your speech may be a bit more direct and blunt and the wrong words may be blurted out accidentally; do be more aware of your speech this year. You may find yourself with communication difficulty in dealing with people, so that is something you need to overcome as well. There are good opportunities for you to meet rich and influential people who can become a benefactor or mentor to you, and also to travel overseas for work related matters. There may be additional stress from people as well, so again, the importance of clear and concise communication is key. In conclusion, if you can endure and learn how to manage your tasks well, you will achieve success!

For children born in 2001 and 2010, this year is a challenging year for them as well. They may meet a mentor to guide them and they may also meet someone that they are particularly attracted to, it may be a time for them to learn about love and relationship. These children may take more risk this year though, talking and communicating about the need for money and business arrangements. They will see success, if only they planned sufficiently and take on correct advises. Finally, there is a great deal of work coming from school and home, which they need to deal with and push through. Perseverance will help them this year.

For people born in 1903, 1912, 1921, 1930, 1939, 1948, 1957, 1966, 1975, 1984 and 1993, this is a year with a lot of anger and frustration for you. Firstly, your business and career is going through a lot of ups and downs, creating a lot of stress and frustration. Secondly, you may find that your expenditure is very quick and fast and the amount gets bigger, so where did the money go? Both of these issues alone can make anyone feel the heat. Some of you may find that you have a heart condition or that your heart condition may worsen, in either case, it will be good to have a medical check-up. You may think that to save your current situation, you would need to take risks and that is only half the truth. In fact you have to take calculated risks and make more inform decisions about your investment. Basically, do not be too rash to making decisions when it concerns both money and work, planning a little can go a long way. Do note, however, that you will have a lot of business or career opportunities at the later part of the year.

For children born in 2002 and 2011, the anger and frustration appears to come from people. There are some family issues that these children may need to face, as well as relationship issues. Especially for those born in 2002, they may find their pocket money is dwindling fast. They may need to learn financial budgeting. Also, they might want to know that, spending on their friends is not always a good idea. Or even on their crush for that matter.

For people born in 1904, 1913, 1922, 1931, 1940, 1949, 1958, 1967, 1976, 1985 and 1994, some of you had your ups and downs in business last year and this year, you are more ready to do what you need to do! You are finally ready to do what you had planned and you will increase your network and be able to meet the necessary people for your plans. Although you may have to be careful as there may be some saboteurs mixed in the crowd, but you should be able to pick them out and protect yourself. However, for the inexperienced folk, you may still be susceptible to these saboteurs so do be careful. Knowing the strength and weakness of your network will help you greatly in achieving success.

For children born in 2003 and 2012, they may face certain family issues that turn them to their friends for solace. They will be angry and emotional but because they engage in so much activity, they may attract a lot of new friends and companion. But as his circle of friends grew, acquaintances will leave as well. There may be instances where a new domestic helper joins the family. In this case, the children should be reminded to be nice and not hurt people's feelings with their direct manner of speech. They may face a situation that they are forced to spend money on people such as treating friends to drinks and food. For those born in 2003, there is increased stress in studying and academics.

For people born in 1900, 1905, 1914, 1923, 1932, 1941, 1950, 1959, 1968, 1977, 1986 and 1995, this year has a lot of stress, tension and frustration for you indeed. Let's just say, the year starts with a high note! With such stress from seemingly everywhere, do pay heed to your family as family issues may abound. You may be too fast in exerting your own principles on others that may infuriate them, especially to your family members. In a worst case scenario, the family issues may lead to divorce. As a consequence, you will need to present yourself accordingly. By the way, do be careful of your speech as there is a higher chance for aggressive speech creating stress and tension when you deal with people. You may even get angry because you cannot seem to get your words across, or that they do not seem to understand you 100%. Regardless of the situation, do learn how to manage your stress and anger and delegate out your task as much as possible to relieve your burden, hopefully helping you to be less busy. This year, you may face an auspicious occasion such as the birth of a child.

For those children born in 2004 and 2013, this is a stressful year for different reasons. These children may experience a lot of movement from place to place, such as a new school, a new class, a new home, etc and this actually creates a lot of stress for them. They get busy looking for opportunities to feel safe, especially when there may be some tension within their family. For the children born in 2004, they may start to keep secrets from their family, friends or teachers. If you know such children, do become their close friend and hope they will feel comfortable enough to tell you a secret. This year may be a year that they have to conduct a lot of presentation and selling and they will see great results.

For people born in 1906, 1915, 1924, 1933, 1942, 1951, 1960, 1969, 1978, 1987 and 1996, there is a lot of expenditure this year. You may also find that some of your expenditure is going into investments and that you should take some calculated risk that may derive a lot of return. You can see investment profits from August to September onwards, so do prepare adequately for this time! The great thing is that this year is actually a successful year for you, so it is a great time for you to achieve your goals. Health wise, there may be a heart condition that may surface this year, so do be aware of possible symptom. This year will be a good year for fast and short contract-related businesses as well, otherwise, your career should be in a very stable and strong entity such as in the government. This year bodes a lot of business opportunities but also couple with a lot of instability and insecurity, so make the right choices to see a lot of success.

For children born in 2000, 2005 and 2014, this year is a stressful year for these children. They need to put in a lot of hard work for themselves in other to succeed. Perhaps it is because they appear to be children who tends to procrastinate, hence their parents will push them harder. Fortunately, with hard work comes success, and they will see results this year. They may get angry and frustrated over the amount of work they have, so offer encouragement as well, not just work alone. Some children may want certain things and may try to convince their parents to buy it for them; they will talk and plan for their money. This in turn forces them to be independent to take some risk to seek out some cash and in doing so make them very busy running around.

For people born in 1907, 1916, 1925, 1934, 1943, 1952, 1961, 1970, 1979, 1988 and 1997, this is the year to bring your plans to fruition! Now is not the time to dilly-dally anymore! It is time to start what you have always desired! You will be able to meet a lot of people and the necessary people who can help you in your success, however, do be aware of any saboteurs among them. Although you may face some dilemmas when it comes to deciding the best option to pick, as well as some relationship and family issues, you will still be able to make it this year. Just be aware of work-life balance and spend equal portions of time between work and family or relationship. For those who are facing legal matters this year, there is someone who will appear and be able to help you in it. This is a time for you to broker and close deals and it will be more effective if the necessary planning is in place and the presentation is well thought out; do not be too hasty in your plan. All in all, this is a great year to start turning your dreams into reality.

For children born in 2006, these children may seem at times impulsive to do what they want to do. Do remind them to slow down and plan carefully the steps to take. Oddly enough, while they may seem impulsive about the things they want, they procrastinate on the necessary work to be done. There is also a possibility of family tension this year. These children can be more sharp-tongued this year, so they may create friendship issues if they are not aware. Do remind them to have manners and to bring them up with goodwill. They may be stressed in their planning but results will generally be good.

For people born in 1908, 1917, 1926, 1935, 1944, 1953, 1962, 1971, 1980, 1989 and 1998, this is a stressful and frustrating year for you. You start 2015 with anger and frustration, which leads to more stress gradually; you will likely be very emotional. Perhaps it is because of the workload, perhaps it is because of the presentations you need to do, perhaps it is the relationship issues you have been having lately, but ultimately (you may not want to admit it) it is because of you. You will tend to be more indecisive in your choices this year and may involve in substantially more communication. You may at times appear to talk too much for your own good. If you find that you need a break to relax and de-stress, do it. Your job may present some travel opportunity for you to work overseas, why not extend a day or two to relax? Take that opportunity for a vacation when it presents itself, you definitely need it. Sometimes, issues arise when there is a communication breakdown or when people talk without thinking, so do be aware of what you say; try not to be too blunt or long winded.

For children born in 2007, there may be some family issues that arise this year that creates a lot of stress and tension. As a result, some of these children may display anger signs, become more mischievous or even have violent tendencies. They can be very direct with their words which can be hurtful to their friends. These children may experience a lot of movement within the family or school, such as changing locations often. Should you encounter such children, please show them that there is someone who cares for them deeply enough. Hopefully, it will calm them down enough to change their behaviour, even if the encounter is just briefly in that year.

For people born in 1909, 1918, 1927, 1936, 1945, 1954, 1963, 1972, 1981, 1990 and 1999, this year is a very interesting year for you. Firstly, you will note that your money is going in and out very fast. Secondly, you may find that your business or career is going up and down very fast as well. Thirdly, you may find that your health is getting poor suddenly, which includes a possible heart issue, among other things. Why is it interesting if it sounds so bad? Well, since you have pre-emptive knowledge of what might occur, then you can prepare for what may occur. It may be a time to take some calculated risk and make some investments at this time for it may bring you massive returns. However, do know when to cut loss if the tide turns against you. You may even need to plan your finances carefully and spend less on unnecessary items. Do have a backup plan in preparation of what may occur with regards to your job. And don't get angry so easily, stay happy and keep your heart in shape. Have a well balance diet and proper good and healthy nutrition as well as exercise! Have a positive mind-set!

For children born in 2008, these children may find that they get temperamental easily this year. They may also start to keep secrets from people as well. Some of them might be planning something secretive. It may be good to let them continue as it is in their character to do so, just ensure they are planning the right thing at the right time. Don't plan a party before exams, for example. However, they do have that impulsiveness for fun and riskiness at this time.

If the number you found was the number 4:

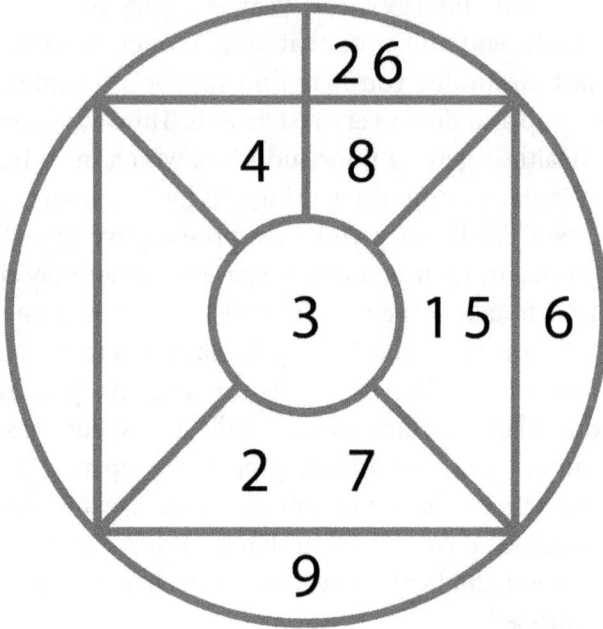

The year starts with a lot of planning be it studies, relationship or even family. However, having put in place such a lot of plans in such a short time and trying to execute them may bring you a lot of stress. The stress may cause you to be more emotional and anger may surface. When you are angry, you are thus prone to fast and aggressive communication and may say the wrong things at the wrong time, you may face a marriage issue due to this. You may see yourself meeting more people and losing contact with others easily this year. Fortunately, the main issues occur in the first half of the year. The second half of the year is a bit better especially when the network you can build can help you in your career and success. For singles, this is a good time for you to get involved in a relationship as well!

For people born in 1901, 1910, 1919, 1928, 1937, 1946, 1955, 1964, 1973, 1982 and 1991, you have to be more aware of the intentions of the network that you build as you may attract saboteurs and backstabbers. You may meet many people this year but they come as fast as they go. Some may attempt to steal your plans and ideas to get ahead of you, just be wary of those who suddenly get very friendly with you. These people can make this year a challenging year for you and they may even have the potential to cause family issues and problems. This will definitely lead you to be angry. Do note that should you be planning alone, let the people around you know about it and some pointers may actually point you to the right direction. Should you decide to go ahead with the plan do also note that you may fare better with a backup plan. You may find some obstacles in your business, so you should really work at finding all ways and means for solutions as well as include them in your plans. However, this year is not without its merits, it has the potential for you to travel overseas for career or business. You may find it difficult to believe, but if you are willing to take some risks into investments, you can make some handsome profits.

Now for children born in 2009, these children may find that this year is a challenging year. There is a lot of movement that may cause them to feel discomfort. They may also discover the thrill and excitement of taking risks and daring to do things by them-selves. Fortunately, they will have the opportunity to grow and learn under someone well-learned and knowledgeable.

For people born in 1902, 1911, 1920, 1929, 1938, 1947, 1956, 1965, 1974, 1983 and 1992, this year is full of stress and frustration for you. The aggression in your speech and the forceful selling that you engage may lead to some issues, it may entail some failed financial planning that you may undertake, so be aware. All that talk about money matters will give you more and more stress. Your work may include presentations, travelling overseas, and may require you to work and work a lot. Fortunately, hard work will truly pay off for you, so endure and persevere through the stressful and frustrating workload, the busy and tiring schedules, and you will see justified returns. However, for some of you, there may be legal matters to settle this year, so just be aware of that issue. One more thing to take note, is to be mindful of what you say, as if you are not careful, you may hurt others when you speak too fast and without thinking. Not to mention the possible fact that there may be miscommunications and misunderstandings. All in all, be mindful of yourself and be positive and endure through this year.

For children born in 2001 and 2010, they are more likely this year to meet someone who can mentor and guide them. However, for the children born in 2001, they may find themselves working harder this year. They may find themselves over spending as well. If you find that they are talking about money and keep asking for money, do offer some advice about financial budgeting and planning their finances wisely. However, if they are trying to make some money for themselves and are taking some risk doing it, do offer some timely advise just in case they falter due to their poor planning. They may meet with an auspicious situation this year or may even have a crush on someone.

For people born in 1903, 1912, 1921, 1930, 1939, 1948, 1957, 1966, 1975, 1984 and 1993, you may experience ups and downs in your job this year, but the good news is this is your lucky year. Someone might appear when you most needed some help and this person may lead you out of your obstacle. If you are still single, a potential relationship partner is likely to appear this year but for those who are married, be careful of ending up with a third party in the marriage. You may also find yourself having higher expenditure than the usual, especially with the amount of meet-ups and increased network you have this year. However, with increased network, you should be wary that one or two of them might want to make use of you instead. You may have a chance of having someone investing money in you as you talk more about money, however, do be careful not to be overly aggressive in your speech. This year is a great year for you to act on your plans, and the year should end on a good note, where you have the potential to see massive success in your endeavours.

For children born in 2002 and 2011, these children may experience increased tension and stress within the family. This year, these children will be meeting a lot of new friends and forming networks. Some of these children will start to understand their friends' strengths and weaknesses better, and will be able to use their capabilities for desired outcomes. With a bit of luck this will allow them to get what they want and achieve their goals in this year.

For people born in 1904, 1913, 1922, 1931, 1940, 1949, 1958, 1967, 1976, 1985 and 1994, there are huge family and relationship problems that may surface for you this year. This may be a big marriage issue that can even lead to divorce; fortunately, there is conflict and relationship management consultation that we provide which can help you both to repair the relationship. There may be a lot of anger and emotional issues that may come to light, whether it is because of the tension within the family or because of the people in the working environment. There may be a saboteur or backstabber appearing this year too, so do be careful and wary. It is understandable that if you are so stressed with dealing with people, it may show as anger to other people. This may cause others to leave you momentarily. Take the stress in stride and delegate out the stress to other people, rewards may be good by doing so. It is not easy dealing with such stressful issues, but do let us know and we can help.

For children born in 2003 and 2012, these children may experience huge family issues this year, especially involving arguments or fights. What is happening in the family, may take its toll on the child, and will likely affect the child in a negative way. These children may find themselves getting angry easily and getting frustrated with their friends too. Some may use violence when interacting with their friends. It will also affect their schoolwork. If you know of such children going through such issues, do offer a helping hand to them.

For people born in 1900, 1905, 1914, 1923, 1932, 1941, 1950, 1959, 1968, 1977, 1986 and 1995, this year is a great year for you to achieve success in your goals! As long as you plan with your goals in mind, and plan each step and process carefully, you will see results this year. Truly, no one can stop you! In addition, you are able to move people with your enthusiasm in your communication and they will be able to help you in your tasks too! Do get these supporters and assign them tasks to their strengths. They will help you a lot this year. You may encounter some rich and influential people this year who may be willing to invest (if you play your cards right). All in all, this is a great year for your career but do spare some time for family matters too. Too much time in your career can cause family problems as well, especially when success is within reach and you want to achieve it at an accelerated rate. Things can be quite busy in your career, but always remember to spend quality time with your family and loved ones.

For those children born in 2004 and 2013, there may be a lot of movement whether it is within the school or about the home. These children may find themselves a bit more secretive this year. Fortunately, for the children born in 2004, they are able to find success in their goals this year, but only if they have decided on what they want to achieve and how to achieve it. With great success comes great rewards, so if you are able to guide them, please do so and assist.

For people born in 1906, 1915, 1924, 1933, 1942, 1951, 1960, 1969, 1978, 1987 and 1996, you might find yourself with high expenditure this year. Although you have taken into account your finances and you are planning it well, you may realize that you still have high expenses. You may need to question the necessity of some of the expenses. Fortunately, your investments will see profit this year, although taking calculated risks will be much better. Always be aware of where your money is going into, and stay away from the bad spots. You also have some potential work opportunity overseas but you may have to venture alone to see greater success. Also, although you have something in mind to start this year, and you have started to build a network as well, you should be careful of the intentions of some people. There may be a saboteur or a backstabber appearing this year, so do be careful. Another thing to take note is a possible heart condition, so have a well-balanced nutrition and take care not to get angry so easily!

For children born in 2000, 2005 and 2014, this year provides new experiences for them. Especially for those born in 2000 and 2005, there is an increased in the amount of studying that they need to do, which increase their stress and work. There may be some presentations that they need to handle too. Even though they seem to need to plan a lot, they need that push and motivation too. They will also need to be careful of being betrayed or make use of by one or two of their friends. They will also need to be aware of their money, as some of their friends might borrow their money and never return.

For people born in 1907, 1916, 1925, 1934, 1943, 1952, 1961, 1970, 1979, 1988 and 1997, this is a great year for you to build your network and achieve rewarding success! You are able to put your plans into actions and this will help you to achieve success. Building that huge network which can help your business is no mean feat either! This huge network of yours can help your business to attain more success, profits and network! However, do be careful of speaking your mind too easily, as with knowing so many people, there is a possibility to offend one or two of them easily. If you have a lifetime of experience, you may be up for mentorship, meaning, you may be offering consultation or advice to people in order to develop and grow them. However, if you are inexperienced, this is a great year for you to seek a mentor to guide you! Also, if you are single, you have opportunity to find a potential relationship partner this year and if you are married, do take heed and avoid unnecessary trouble. Lastly, you may find yourself talking a lot about money so do be aware that some people do avoid this topic.

For children born in 2006, these children may find crushes happening this year. These children may not like to plan that much, and in this year, you may find that they do their plans and schedules unbelievably fast, you are not sure whether they put deep thought into their planning process. They are more ready to do the actions as compared to planning, which is why they seem to rush through. Hence, do offer some guidance if you know of such children in the planning phase of a project, or doing their study schedule. Another thing you might note is that these children are communicating more and more, such that sometimes during such a planning process, for example, they might be talking more than planning.

For people born in 1908, 1917, 1926, 1935, 1944, 1953, 1962, 1971, 1980, 1989 and 1998, this year is a stressful and frustrating year for you. Problems seem to come from all sides and areas. Other than from work, family issues also abound. You have to be careful this year as if the issues escalate, there may be talk of divorce. There are a lot of negative emotions this year, such as anger, sadness, frustration and agitation. All these internal feelings can be seen externally through physical displays and communicative words. So you will also need to be wary of what you say, and you may hurt your friends and family by accident. Be aware of how you present yourself to others, and maintain a calm demeanour when speaking. Usually in the face of such situations, you may seek out new relationships and new friends, and especially if you are single, you may seek out new relationships as a means to find comfort. Seeking advice from others can help you in relationship conflicts, but do note to seek advice from the right people!

For children born in 2007, these children may experience escalating family issues that is hard to ignore. These issues can cause the children to vent their stress and frustration elsewhere, unintentionally hurting their friends in school. This year also happens to be a year where they meet and make a lot of new friends, so it will be crucial for them to seek proper support should they require it. These children will normally keep things in their chest, but this can cause further problems, hence, it will be important for you to get the right help for these children when you notice them.

For people born in 1909, 1918, 1927, 1936, 1945, 1954, 1963, 1972, 1981, 1990 and 1999, there is some expenditure this year that requires you to spend and spend. There are also some ups and downs in your job, which may include some stress with planning and schedules. You may also experience some stress with money. Fortunately, you can take calculated risks in doing investments that should yield handsome rewards. However, should you decide to keep such unstable career matters from your significant other, it may cause undue relationship stress and tension. Hence, it may be a good idea to discuss what is happening with your significant other. If you are still single though, sadly, this is not a good year for you to get a relationship partner, it may be better for you to focus on your career first. Relationship for you can create a lot of tension this year. However, if you truly want to get one, do let us know and we can see how we can assist.

For children born in 2008, these children are usually quite stubborn, and this year shows as they can get more and more secretive. However, see it as if they are becoming more independent and aware of their surroundings. Their families may have some minor issues occurring and these children will not let anyone know.

If the number you found was the number 5:

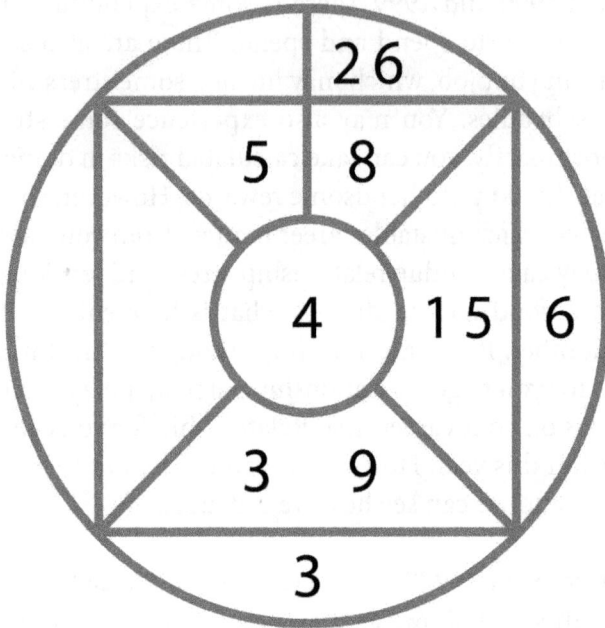

Last year's stress loads has continued into this year, so you have a lot to handle. These challenges create more stress and frustration and may create more problems. Know that you are stressed and take time-out, otherwise you may end up bringing the stress into your family and inadvertently create issues and tension in the marriage. The worst case scenario is to start talking about divorce! There may be tension in a relationship as well, and this may lead to a breakup. You may be stressed with planning and scheduling, especially when you have to plan fast for business or career, because your job or business may be a little wobbly ahead. It will be a good idea to consider short term business or contracts based work and persevere to see light at the end of the tunnel.

For people born in 1901, 1910, 1919, 1928, 1937, 1946, 1955, 1964, 1973, 1982 and 1991, this year you will be meeting a lot of people and building your network. However, you have to be careful and wary of their intentions for the connection and newfound relationship. Some of them might want to use your for their own purposes, which may not benefit you at all. Although you may see some financial profit to be made, the advice is to tread lightly. Since you can build a huge network this year, if you can pick your supporters and people, which will be much better, although you may need another person to offer another point of view to decide the people you want to be connected with. Offer to spend some money on such great supporters (such as a drink or a meal) and you can see good begets good. Present yourself in a well manner and there may be opportunities to travel overseas for business. Do also be aware that while your business may be improving, you need to maintain a work-life balance. If you do not spend enough time with your family or significant other, and spend too much time socializing or in your job, you may find some relationship issues and tension arising. So do know when to separate time for work and for family.

Now for children born in 2009, they will find and make a lot of new friends this year. They will also meet someone who can mentor and guide them well. However, this year can be an emotional year for these children. These children can be quite stubborn or hard-headed and you may find them to be more responsive and vocal when they are conversing about what they want. There may be a lot of movement whether it is the house or the school or class as well but these children should be able to handle the change easily.

For people born in 1902, 1911, 1920, 1929, 1938, 1947, 1956, 1965, 1974, 1983 and 1992, this year is a year of networking as well as opportunities to travel overseas for business. However, all these can cause you to be busy moving around and may create some stress and tension. Do be aware to remain calm in the face of challenges, being angry or frustrated and saying hurtful things does not help you find a solution. Your business this year may be fast and short term, like a contract-based business. Among your network, you may meet rich and influential people and when you talk to these people, you have to be careful for you may accidentally offend someone this year. That may cause a chain reaction that results in someone sabotaging your job or personal life. However, meeting the right people of influence can help move your business in better areas of success. Hence, select the right people to build connections with, and be mindful of what you say, doing so will help you to achieve success in your career this year.

For children born in 2001 and 2010, these children will be building a lot of friendships this year. Especially for those children born in 2001, there will be a lot of exchange of advice between them, whether it's a mentor giving them advice, or they give advice to their friends. They have to be mindful of long term goals and know the necessary steps to take, otherwise their moments of success is short-lived. They may be taking some risks in some matters, such as asking their crush out, in which case, they need to know that any failure is still an opportunity for experience.

For people born in 1903, 1912, 1921, 1930, 1939, 1948, 1957, 1966, 1975, 1984 and 1993, you have to be very careful this year. Your job may be unstable and have a lot of ups and downs which causes you stress and tension. Maintain your composure and refrain from displaying bursts of anger. Try to find some other ways to relieve stress and tension as well as to relieve anger. If you are not careful, that may aggravate and cause a heart condition. Such negative emotions may also cause some tension in your relationship or family. There are also signs of high and fast expenditure which you may need to be wary of, whether such expenses are necessary or not. Be aware of expenditure as a means to relieve stress and negative emotions as that can create financial issues instead. Doing and following financial budgeting is good in such situations. You may also have to present yourself articulately in a manner to showcase your abilities and capabilities as well as act on your plans to ensure success. Maintaining a calm demeanour is key for both your career and relationships. Persevere through this year and it will help you to be a better person with greater experience for future situations!

For children born in 2002 and 2011, there may be a lot of stress and tension this year. These children may experience family situations which create tension, and these children may learn such behaviour and display in other situations. Overall the friendships in school may be strained if they do not learn the right behaviour or the right ways to relieve negative emotions. Fortunately, this year may present a situation where they meet someone who can guide them through the rough situation. However, whether they choose the right mentor is up to them, the chosen mentor may put them on the right path or the left path. They may be indecisive initially, but once chosen, these children may be hard-headed and not change their mentor.

For people born in 1904, 1913, 1922, 1931, 1940, 1949, 1958, 1967, 1976, 1985 and 1994, you can see some success this year! Your willingness to work and do things has allowed you to see some results this year. However, you may have to be careful as some people may not like how you do things, this results in attracting some backstabbers or saboteurs. Thus, you have to learn to plan each step towards your goals with backup plans for possible hiccups, as well as to be ready for any unforeseen circumstances. You may also consider seeking advice from individuals who have done it before in order to gain some additional knowledge and knowhow. Only then, can no one stop you from achieving your full rewards. Having such great plans for business allows you to attract people to participate in the same success that you achieve. Teaching others who to achieve their own success is a great thing to add to your portfolio this year as well! However, while your career seems fruitful, you need to be careful of possible problems in other areas of life.

For children born in 2003 and 2012, this year is a tricky year for them. In terms of academics, most of these children are able to handle it well and can excel very well too. Therefore, most of these children will see their success and attain what they want. However, there are some family issues that may occur at home and these children will not want others to know about. Some of these children may have these issues affect their academics though. These children can be pretty strong-willed at times, but can be very emotional at other times. It is when they choose to display such emotions, can it be possible for someone to help and assist them.

For people born in 1900, 1905, 1914, 1923, 1932, 1941, 1950, 1959, 1968, 1977, 1986 and 1995, this year is filled with challenges and obstacles that you need to overcome to get what you want. You have to be vocal enough to get people to move and yet subtle enough that they don't feel threaten or hurt. This is one of those trying years where you can be quite stressed out dealing with people too. Some of you may experience a change of job while others will receive opportunities to go overseas for business. You will experience stress from all over and may need to work overtime. If you are able to delegate some of your work to others to help you, that will be very good for you. You may also experience financial stress and difficulties as your money goes in and out very fast in a blink of an eye. However, you may meet a rich and influential person who can be your mentor, so learn from the best person you meet! In addition, you have to be careful as you may get an accident or require an operation this year, hence, do ensure you have enough savings or insurance coverage. Endure through and you can become a stronger individual!

For those children born in 2004 and 2013, there may be a lot of movement and changes in the environment whether it is for school or for the home. There are quite a few challenges for these children to experience and go through this year too. This can be a very emotional and trying year for them. They need to learn to be independent this year.

For people born in 1906, 1915, 1924, 1933, 1942, 1951, 1960, 1969, 1978, 1987 and 1996, this year brings some financial difficulties. You may find yourself spending your finances too fast or someone is spending them too fast, and this can create some issues with money. There are some investments which, if you calculate the risk before you venture into it, should see some profits and returns. All this money talk can stress people, whether it is your colleagues and subordinates, or friends and family, and while the stress on the family is not too good, the stress on your colleagues or subordinates can help to move them to complete tasks on time. Just be mindful not to stress them too much, rather, motivate them with words and encouragement will be the best way to go. Once your business kicks off again, clients and customers will come back and increase in number too. With an increase of people coming to you, you will increase your network and have the opportunities to meet people who can help you as well. Sharing your business ideas with such people is bound to create your own career path in the best possible way!

For children born in 2000, 2005 and 2014, this year will introduce new friends to these children. However, as these children are easily temperamental, it can cause emotional issues or stress and tension issues in the family and in social relationships. This year is stressful for the children born in 2000 and 2005, whether in school and flooded by school work, or whether due to the emotional issues created in the family, or possible relationship strains with their friends. If you know of such children, do be there for them and support them as well as to teach them how to manage their stress and emotions.

For people born in 1907, 1916, 1925, 1934, 1943, 1952, 1961, 1970, 1979, 1988 and 1997, this year is a great year for networking. Since you more or less have an idea of what you want to do, you are prepared for bringing in people to assist you. However, while you may meet rich and influential people who can be your benefactor or mentor, there are also possibilities to meet people who may not want the best for you. This is because when you build up your network, you meet both good and not so good people. But do get some advice from the people who done it before and have attained their own success as well, it will greatly help in your planning and actions to take. Generally, you will be able to attain your success, if you find the right people amongst your network to assist you in the right jobs. There will be a lot of actions to be done this year, although some people may not approve your actions, creating stress and tension. It is definitely a busy and stressful year when you are trying to make everything fall in place and when there is so much to be done. Do note of possible legal actions this year. Persevere and you will see your success this year.

For children born in 2006, these children will meet a lot of people too, from someone who can guide them, to increasing their social network. However, this year may have some anger issues arising, which cause them to be sharp-tongued at times, and may also strain their friendships and other relationships with people. If you are the person guiding such children, so spend some time advising on how to manage their emotions and stress. This year also brings some stress and frustration to these children.

For people born in 1908, 1917, 1926, 1935, 1944, 1953, 1962, 1971, 1980, 1989 and 1998, this year is very stressful and frustrating for you. All the stress seems to come from everywhere! Your job seems to have stress from schedules and deadlines and plans as well as being very fast-paced and unstable, your family also has some increase in stress and tension, which you have to be careful because there may also be talk of divorce! You don't need any additional stress from your significant other with the deadline for that presentation, now don't you? However, work-life balance is important and family is very important too. One good advice will be for you to take a break from work and go on vacation or have a talk with your significant other to discuss appropriately the issues. Once you solve this issue, the work related issues can be gradually resolved as well. One more thing, don't let your anger get ahead of yourself, anger will only escalate matters into much worse situations, whether it is in your job or in your family or even in social situations. Maintain a calm demeanour and present yourself in a manner befitting of what you want to achieve. This year is really all about what you show to others. Plan carefully and act on it!

For children born in 2007, these children may have family issues arising which includes arguments and even fights. The emotional stress may cause them to act violently both at home and in school. However, these children will not want to tell anyone about it, so if you know of such children, you need to just be there for them when things go south. One of the tell-take signs is when they seem to get angry or frustrated more easily, so do watch out for these signs, and especially when they hit someone.

For people born in 1909, 1918, 1927, 1936, 1945, 1954, 1963, 1972, 1981, 1990 and 1999, this year is full of challenges for you to overcome and become stronger! Such challenges include and are not restricted to health, work, family, financial, personal and emotional issues, social and environmental issues, etc, so please prepare yourself appropriately. You can get some profits from investments but do some calculated risk management before going into such investments in order to maximise the potential profits. There may be some instability in your job so do get ready for what may occur, such as a change in the job scope or the sudden overseas business trip. Do take care should you receive such business opportunities because this year also has some indication for accidents or injuries, so do be wary and ensure you have adequate insurance coverage for accidents and health. In the worse possible scenario, some of you may be hospitalized or even require an operation. This can be a taxing year but do keep yourself together and endure through such an experience to grow and develop from it.

For children born in 2008, this year is full of movement and challenges for these children which they have to acknowledge and have support to go through. There is a change in environment, a new place, where they need to get accustomed to; some may not get accustomed to it and may get all emotional while others can get used to the environment pretty well. These children will also receive school work that is quite challenging, and so they need to learn as fast as possible under a great mentor. There may also be some secrets that these children are learning how to keep to themselves, but it shows that they are learning to be more independent.

If the number you found was the number 6:

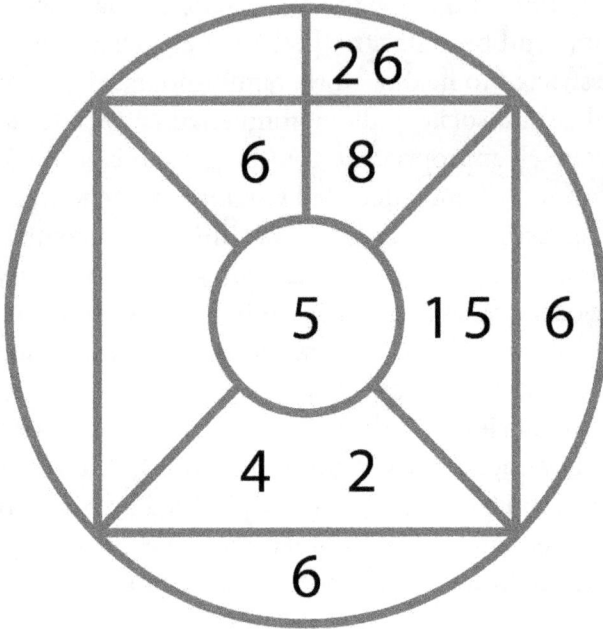

This year may have more obstacles in the way, you may need to face some financial issues and may lead you to be stressed with money. Such issues are part and parcel of life and you should strive to keep your finances in check before it leads you to more serious situations, such as a strain in the marriage. Due to the strain in finances, you may be forced to be more prudent with your spending and may cause you to be more emotional. Hence, you should make proper plans, especially your finances, and communicate your plans and problems with people you trust. Once that is taken care of, you need to get busy and moving! Ensuring all your necessary items are moving in the right direction needs a lot of work but once all is in place, no one can stop you from achieving!

For people born in 1901, 1910, 1919, 1928, 1937, 1946, 1955, 1964, 1973, 1982 and 1991, there is a lot of networking this year for you but do take heed that with so much networking done, you can attract both good and not so good network. Hence, do be careful of other people's intentions as some may make use of you while others may cause you to have family disputes and even to the extent of legal issues. Overall, interacting with people can sometimes create more issues than solve them. However, once you find the right people you can truly set things in motion and achieve what you need to achieve this year. Seek advice from the right people, the people who has done it before and achieve their own success, and learn from these people. Things will truly get busy in the latter half of the year and you have to ensure your schedules are in order. You can consider settling your schedules as early as the start of the year so that you know your plans are moving in the best possible direction. Remember, the key for this year is to build a good network of supporters!

For children born in 2009, they may getting more emotional this year, especially over the smallest of things. Emotions such as sadness or anger can be commonplace. These negative emotions may be the result of family issues that may be happening at home. Some however, may experience such emotions when dealing with their friends; their friends may be doing things that create tension and stress. They will need the guidance of a good mentor to support them in their time of need as well as to teach them life skills on dealing with stress and inappropriate behaviour.

For people born in 1902, 1911, 1920, 1929, 1938, 1947, 1956, 1965, 1974, 1983 and 1992, this year has a lot of stressful challenges for you. Money has being an issue more times that appropriate and this year is no different. One thing for consideration are the business opportunities overseas that you may be going for this year, some of you can afford going overseas but some of you have other commitments back at home. It is one of those work-life balance that you need to consider carefully. You should also be careful of not letting the stress and tension from work get into your personal life as that may affect your communication with your family and significant other, social life and friends. Be careful of what you say to people this year and that should reduce potential conflict from occurring or even escalating, such as divorce or legal matters. This year is indeed a stressful and trying time and requires you to input a lot of hard work, but enduring through and planning things carefully will help you as well as develop you into a better individual!

For children born in 2001 and 2010, these children may face some emotional stress this year which cause them to seek out people for reassurance. Thus, these children may develop a dependency on their family or friends if they are not careful. They may be some movement involved such as moving house or changing school, or the introduction of a new environment. The new environment may cause some excitement or even anxicty which will increase the chance for seeking new friendships and bonds. All in all, this can be an interesting year for these children.

For people born in 1903, 1912, 1921, 1930, 1939, 1948, 1957, 1966, 1975, 1984 and 1993, this year is full of ups and downs for your career. Talk about a fast and furious job! It is quite unstable this year and you may actually consider a change of job or doing even more jobs but this will make you very busy and possibly angry. However, if your career deals with short term contracts then this is a good year for you. This year also has some risky investments which you can see profits if you had done some calculated risk management. Your finances also appear unstable as there is also a lot of expenditure for you this year either by yourself or by someone else. Some proper financial budgeting might be in order. You may want to take care of your health and be wary of potential signs of a heart issue occurring this year. Try to maintain a work-life balance as well otherwise, there may be some relationship and family issues occurring. Most of the issues is actually from your career so upon solving that, things will fall into place more naturally.

For children born in 2002 and 2011, this year is a year of issues within the family. Fortunately, the issues are still rather small however, as these children are emotional children, they may let it get to them. For the children born in 2002, they may let the family issues affect their work, resulting in them needing tuition. They can meet a lot of people this year and tutors are part of the people they can meet. However, some of them might be spending money as a means to relieve their stress, so they may find themselves with a lot of unnecessary expenditure. All in all, this year can be successful for them if they put in effort to achieve their desired results.

For people born in 1904, 1913, 1922, 1931, 1940, 1949, 1958, 1967, 1976, 1985 and 1994, this year is a bit complicating for you. On one hand you can meet a lot of rich and influential people who can be your benefactor or mentor yet on the other hand you may attract backstabbers and saboteurs. Be aware of the intentions of the people around you, learn to avoid the ones that do you harm and learn from the ones who do you good. Knowing their character and personality as well as seeking the right people will assist you greatly this year. You may have guidance on leadership roles and on organization skills, but do be careful with your actions and plans as they may have unforeseen consequences. There may be some movement this year, whether it is an overseas business opportunities or a change in the work environment. In the early half of the year, it will be a good time to set some time for financial budgeting, especially when a big event is due to happen. Except for the problems with people, this year is still pretty good in terms of your career and happiness.

For children born in 2003 and 2012, there may be some family dispute occurring in their families this year. This will require them to seek out a mentor or a guide to teach them how to better manage their emotions and behaviour. Fortunately, for the children born in 2003, their academic are still quite ok and should not be affected by their emotional state that much. However, should the family issues escalate and cause them undesired stress and tension, then their academics might become affected. Hence, if these are your children, do ensure your family issues do not escalate.

For people born in 1900, 1905, 1914, 1923, 1932, 1941, 1950, 1959, 1968, 1977, 1986 and 1995, this year will involve a lot of communication to get what you need and what you want. Firstly, you need to re-establish your network of supporters by seeking them out and communicating to them what you aim to do for yourself or for your company. After which, you can communicate to them your desired outcomes to your supporters so that they can assist you in the best way possible. Combining these two methods is the best way for you to get people moving in the right direction that you need them to go. Hence, you need to be careful with the words you use, you should not appear too aggressive and should not be unkind with your words, aim to make friends not enemies. With so much communication happening, there may be instances of negative feedback and then they might be some issues when you deal with these people. You may be reluctant or lack confidence, but there is someone who should appear this year to help you with such methods of communication. Although you are focused in your career this year, do spare some quality time with family and loved ones, otherwise, some family issue might escalate. Another issue that you may have is with finances, how you earn your money and how you spend it is key this year. Play your cards right, and all will be fine.

For those children born in 2004 and 2013, there are opportunities to meet and make a lot of friends, especially if there is a lot of movement or change in environment. However, in the earlier half of the year, these children may get a bit emotional and this may cause issues in saying what they mean, which leads to communication breakdown. They need to familiarize how to speak properly to people so that there is less stress in communicating what is on their mind. If not careful, it may end up them not speaking their mind at all, thus keeping things to themselves, both positive and negative.

For people born in 1906, 1915, 1924, 1933, 1942, 1951, 1960, 1969, 1978, 1987 and 1996, this year has a lot of financial issues that you need to take care of, both the money coming in and the money going out. Since you have knowledge of it now, do take some time to do some proper financial budgeting and stick to it for 2015, otherwise you may find your losses are amazing! There is some potential profits to be made through investments but do some risk management first before going into it. Another issue is that your job may be a bit unstable this year because there are a lot of ups and downs and issues may arise. Also, do note that your heart is a bit weak this year, hence, it will be good to have an exercise plan and proper nutrition prepared for 2015. Be aware of your emotions and remain calm in the face of such challenges. This can be an emotional and trying year. It is easy to let go but remaining strong is what you need to do this year!

For children born in 2000, 2005 and 2014, it is an emotional year for these children. Especially for those born in 2000 and 2005, this year is a stressful and frustrating year for them. They may find that their academics are much harder and there is so much to learn, they feel that they cannot cope sufficiently with the system. You may see their results is not constant, and if so, do ensure these children have a good break and relax their brain before studying again. The stress needs to be properly taken care of before they can continue their academics.

For people born in 1907, 1916, 1925, 1934, 1943, 1952, 1961, 1970, 1979, 1988 and 1997, this year requires you to meet a lot of people. Once you settled your plans, go and seek out these people who can assist you, and avoid those who may do more harm than good. This is an interesting year where you have the opportunity to meet a potential partner, this is great news for single persons whereas married persons should be careful not to get involved in such matters. You may also consider hiring some people who excel in planning and organization to assist you. This is a great year for you to learn from successful people or to impart your skills and knowledge to other people for them to attain their own success. Once you got the right people doing the right job, it is time for you to showcase and present to potential clients! Do plan carefully what you want to say and everything will be fine. Also, try not to think and plan too much, rather act on your plans in order to get started. Your success is within grasp, so reach out and take it with your own hands!

For children born in 2006, this year will bring a lot of new people into their lives, however, these children need to know when to hold their tongue and when to speak, otherwise, they may un-intentionally say the wrong thing at the wrong time. Especially when they are meeting new friends for the first time, first impression is everything, and it could mean the difference between a new friend and a new foe. These children are very creative and have their own way of thinking so if they insist on continuing their behaviour, well, don't push them.

For people born in 1908, 1917, 1926, 1935, 1944, 1953, 1962, 1971, 1980, 1989 and 1998, this is a challenging and trying time for you. This year has challenges and obstacles that can bring you stress and frustration. From work to family, from social life to health issues, it seems like anything is possible to occur this year. Your relationship issues may escalate due to your emotional state and how you communicate, so be mindful of your words and be aware of your emotions. Indeed, stress and frustration can cause more hurtful words but this is where you need to remain strong. Most of the other issues will involve money, so do ensure that your finances are in order. If you are in need of money, do seek legitimate sources of income. Illegal methods will always bring more harm to you and your loved ones. Also ensure that your insurance coverage is able to cover what may occur (such as health issues and accidents) this year. This year, and especially in the latter half of the year, you may have to present yourself and articulate your thoughts in a manner that allows you to win people and their hearts. When you are able to do so, truly no one can stop you from achieving what you desire. This is something you must remember for this year.

For children born in 2007, the family that these children belong to may be experiencing some issues at home. This can cause unnecessary stress and tension in the children, especially when these children are so emotional. Such negative emotions may influence these children in unpredictable ways, and cause future problems for themselves. Some of these children may still be able to cope with their studies while others may succumb to their negative emotions and it can show in their lack of attention or behavioural issues. Do look out for these children and try to help them when you can.

For people born in 1909, 1918, 1927, 1936, 1945, 1954, 1963, 1972, 1981, 1990 and 1999, this year is a year of money! But a year of money can be both good and bad. You may experience a lot of ups and downs with your finances so do be aware of your expenditure and where it goes to. Some financial budgeting may help keep your money in your pockets. There is also opportunities for investments that you may see profits but having some calculated risk will help you see better rewards. Your career or business may start to get more fast-paced this year. Such instability in your career may cause you to take riskier investments, but it is more advisable to plan ahead. You may want to be careful as you may experience some accident or health issue this year. Do ensure that you have adequate and proper insurance coverage for any possible health or accident issue. It can be as small as a health scare, to as big as an actual accident that requires an operation.

For children born in 2008, this year is an emotional year for them. It is also a year where they may experience more falls, accidents and injuries. Do ensure that these children have good nutrition and are well taken care of for their health. There is some instability with their academics as they need to get used to the education system.

If the number you found was the number 7:

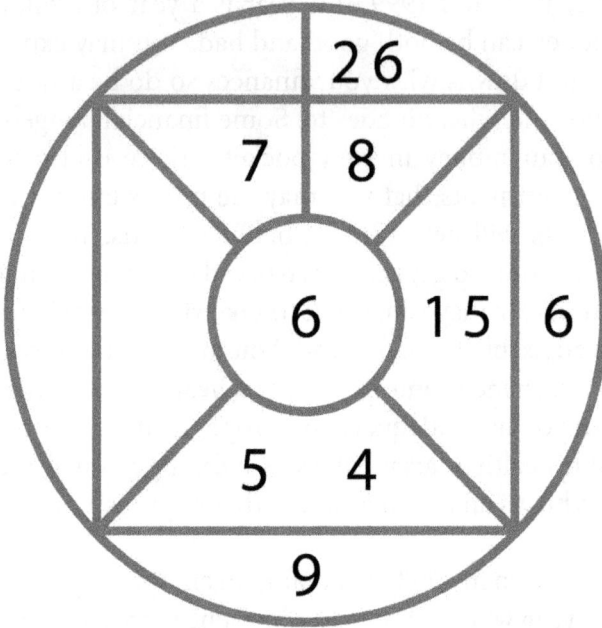

You begin the year meeting many people and form a good network; however, people may come and go very fast as well. Within your network, you may meet with people who will give you a lot of stress and tension, but you need to endure this stress to see your returns. You are likely to spend more money managing your network leading to more stress in your finances. For the stress from people who are constantly in your lives, you need to endure as well because there is a goal at the end that you are looking to achieve. Manage and plan your expenditure and persevere to see your plan through, and truly no one can stop you from achieving your desired outcomes!

For people born in 1901, 1910, 1919, 1928, 1937, 1946, 1955, 1964, 1973, 1982 and 1991, you really have to be aware of the people and network that you have as this year, you will attract backstabbers and saboteurs. It will be ideal to choose the network that you want, before you build it up, and seek the right people for it. That way, you can save yourself some problems and troubles later in the year. You have quite some work cut out for you this year, with all the work in your career or business, you may even need to do some overtime in some areas. This year is also a bit stressful, after dealing with so many people, you may also suffer some family issues as well as internal emotional conflict. There is also financial stress that you have to endure. Indeed, this year you may have to make a hard choice. There is also the possibility of some legal matters that you need to resolve this year. After going through so much and working so hard, it is fortunate that the latter half of the year brings success in your endeavours! Good things truly come to those who wait and persevere!

Now for children born in 2009, they may find a mentor or a guide this year who can help them and teach them. Some of the guidance that they need is in the social life and friendships. These children are generally quite nice and compassionate children, although at times, they may seem a bit greedy. This greediness may cause them their friendships, although admittedly, such friendships are easily regained when lost, especially at this age.

For people born in 1902, 1911, 1920, 1929, 1938, 1947, 1956, 1965, 1974, 1983 and 1992, this year is a great year for you to network and gather supporters! Not to mention the potential for you to build a network overseas! What has happened is that this year, for some of you, your job or career will provide opportunities for you to travel overseas for business, but whether you decide to take it up or not is entirely up to you. For others, you may experience a change in job and location which allows you to build another network as well. All in all, gathering these supporters is key to your success and what you want to achieve this year. Of course, this year has its fair share of issues for you to handle, creating all the stress and frustration and making you so busy and possibly even running around to handle matters! Such negative influences may cause you to be too straightforward, hence, do be aware of what you intend to say and what comes out. Do also delegate your work to the right people, the right supporters, in order to lessen your workload and stress, especially if you took up a new job scope. All in all, seek the right people, speak the right words, and gather more support for your success!

For children born in 2001 and 2010, this year revolves around friendships and the social circle. Such children have to be mindful and aware that all the friendships they make may not be entirely good, and this is where proper guidance is much needed. Being surrounded by so many others, these children may succumb to peer pressure and cause them to do risky behaviours or tasks, causing them to do something which they normally do not do. Especially for the children born in 2001, they have to be especially careful not to succumb to such negative peer pressure. Other than that, this year is pretty good for their academics.

For people born in 1903, 1912, 1921, 1930, 1939, 1948, 1957, 1966, 1975, 1984 and 1993, you have to be especially careful this year. This year, your job may have ups and downs, causing you much distress and anguish. Did you also know that someone may have sabotage you? Another issue is within the home and family, possibly because of the high expenditure that you allow to happen. After going through so much, you may find that your friends are leaving you behind. One tip will be to better manage your finances in an appropriate manner, thus reducing the unnecessary expenditure. Handle home conflicts in a calm and composed manner and remember to draw a line between work and family, never let them cross the line. Be careful of escalating a heart condition. You cannot deal with any backstabbers or saboteurs, so just ignore and be even happier to show them that you have not lost. There is some possibility of a legal affair occurring so do be aware. Endure and persevere through this difficult year and show what a strong person you are!

For children born in 2002 and 2011, they may experience some family difficulties this year. These children can be quite emotional and this may cause some of their friends to leave them. Some of these children may even get bullied due to their passive nature. This is where new friendships and stronger bonds need to take place. Such children may also seek help from experienced professionals to learn how to handle stress. However, if you spot such children, do offer your assistance to them if you think they need your help.

For people born in 1904, 1913, 1922, 1931, 1940, 1949, 1958, 1967, 1976, 1985 and 1994, this year introduces new friends and network for you. You may also meet a benefactor or mentor who can guide and advice you on the right methods for success and personal development. Some of you may be teaching others in personal development as well, and this will help solidify your value. If you are single, you may also meet your potential partner this year; although for the married, please avoid unnecessary trouble. One thing to note is not to be too rash and impulsive and rush to do what you have planned. It will be risky to do so and unless you have calculated for such a method, it is advisable to plan ahead. Once you have assess the risk management, as well as plan with a goal in mind, you are likely to reap great rewards! You may also attract saboteurs this year, especially since you have planned your path and are moving in the right direction with the help of an experienced person. These people will do you more harm than good. Lastly, know your material well so that you can present your ideas to people in order to win their trust and hearts. This is key to your success!

For children born in 2003 and 2012, this year is a good year for studying and learning. However, there are some family issues that may occur this year. Especially for children born in 2003, this may cause such children to seek out new friendships and decide to separate from the family. Some of their friends may have a negative influence and cause them to engage in risky and negative behaviour. These children need to be under the guidance of an experienced professional who can assist them and be there in their time of need.

For people born in 1900, 1905, 1914, 1923, 1932, 1941, 1950, 1959, 1968, 1977, 1986 and 1995, this year, you have to be careful with your choice of words and how you put your points across. Being articulate is one thing, having the right tonality, expression and energy is something else. When done right, you attract supporters which include the rich and influential, but if done wrong, you may offend some people who may go against you. Having such supporters can assist you in many ways, especially if you assign the right task to the right person. Being able to have such people helping you can assist to achieve success that much faster. Having people who may do you more harm than good, will cause unnecessary anger and tension, and in the worst case scenario, create new legal matters for you. Maintain a calm composure as you carry out your tasks. There is some escalation of family issues as well. Another point to note, is that there is some indication of a heart issue this year, so please do be aware. This year requires that you put in a lot of effort and hard work, which may cause you some stress, but use that stress to motivate yourself!

For children born in 2004 and 2013, they may attract quite a fair bit of poor company and negative influence this year. Especially for the children born in 2004, some of their friends may be a negative influence on them, however unintentionally. Such children will need to learn how to avoid such friends and put in their effort to persevere towards their goals. They can see their success come to fruition only if they do the necessary hard work.

For people born in 1906, 1915, 1924, 1933, 1942, 1951, 1960, 1969, 1978, 1987 and 1996, this year is a great year for you to achieve your success and attain what you want! However, there are some requirements for you to attain the results you want. Firstly, you need to plan carefully the steps as well have an outcome or goal that your supporters know about. Next, you need to get the right people to do the right job. Finally, there are some risks that you have to take but take the calculated risks with the most benefits! You may find yourself having quite a bit of expenditure in the beginning of the year but rest assure that the year will play itself out nicely. You will also find that your investments will yield handsome rewards when the time comes! In addition, this is a great year for you to teach and plan for others. You may find that there are more people who enjoy your presentations and company this year as well. A gentle reminder for you to plan carefully and have a backup plan in case of hiccups, finding the right people to carry out your tasks and you will reap the rewards at the end of the year!

For children born in 2000, 2005 and 2014, this year is a good year where they can see their wants and needs being met. Although it may seem like a stressful year where they need to work and learn, the overall outcome will be very beneficial for them. One of the key takeaways for them this year is that they will learn how to articulate themselves in such a manner than is more understandable and to the point. This will assist them greatly in getting what they want this year.

For people born in 1907, 1916, 1925, 1934, 1943, 1952, 1961, 1970, 1979, 1988 and 1997, you will be meeting a lot of people this year, and while some are good, some are also not so good. What happens is that you need to be more aware of people's true intentions when they decide to network with you, this can help you to ascertain who are the right people to network and who to avoid. It can be quite frustrating when dealing with the aftermath of the problems caused by such people. The good news is that this year is a great year for you to attain success! Hence, your actions and plans need to be in sync, and with the right people gathered, your success is within reach. There is even the opportunity to travel overseas for business that will be presented to you, but it is your choice whether to take it or not. Choose your goals wisely, this year is truly a great year to achieve your goals! A couple of things to take note, you have to be careful as there is some indication of a heart issue arising this year, and there may be some trouble occurring in the middle of the year. Hence, please know the people around you well, so that you know who can help you in your time of need.

For children born in 2006, they will be meeting and making a lot of new friends this year. These children however, may be susceptible to speaking their mind and thus, they may accidentally offend some people with their speech. This will cause some friends to talk bad about them, so they need to be careful with what they say. This year is not easy, there is a lot of feelings of anger and frustration for these children this year. These children are naturally emotional and thus, in touch with their feelings. This can cause them to be direct at times, as a way of dealing with their emotions. Thus, they need to learn how to handle their emotions, especially with upcoming feelings of anger, this year.

For people born in 1908, 1917, 1926, 1935, 1944, 1953, 1962, 1971, 1980, 1989 and 1998, people will cause a lot of stress and frustration this year. Dealing and managing such people can be a bit of a headache but someone has to do it in the end. Therefore, you need to learn how to present yourself in an articulate manner that can appease these people, whether they are your bosses, colleagues, subordinates, or customers. Otherwise, the stress that affects you can affect your family and family issues can arise. You may also feel some financial stress and burden, you may start to look for alternative sources of income. Handle this stress well, and you will see your just rewards. Learning how to maintain calm and composed is also a good skill to build. Fortunately, the latter half of the year is much better, with you being able to plan your path to your goals as well as the solutions to your problems. Truly, another skill that you can develop is the precision in planning the route to get to the end. Thus, no one can stop you from attaining what you rightfully deserve!

For children born in 2007, this year has a lot of stress being caused by people around these children, from both friends and family. This can cause feelings of anguish and frustration in these children, hence they need to learn how to manage their negative emotions. Some of them are able to put their motivation into their academics more due to this stress, which is good for these children. The other children may allow the stress to get to them and you can see that it will affect their academics such as, falling grades, reluctant to do work, don't want to go school, etc. For these children, managing the issues is key for them to succeed this year.

For people born in 1909, 1918, 1927, 1936, 1945, 1954, 1963, 1972, 1981, 1990 and 1999, this year will be an amazing year for you! True, you may see some ups and downs in your job, but the moment you get the right people to support your business and give business to you, you will see your business pick up pretty fast! There may be some expenditure that you need to settle, as well as some investments that may seem risky to take, but approach these investments with caution so that it is relatively safe and more profitable. One thing you have to be aware of is that with such good business throughout the year, you may attract unwanted attention from people who might not share the same view for your success. Therefore, always go about your business and life with a good heart and people will find it difficult to do you any harm. The problems this year seem manageable as you know the people who can help you in such problems, and even if you do not know such people, these people who can help you will "magically" appear just when you need them the most. Knowing the capabilities of the people around you is also a key factor to develop this year, as it will be useful in delegating tasks to the right people when the time comes.

For children born in 2008, these children may attract a lot of friends during their academic time in school as well as during other work involvement. Some of these children will excel well in academics, which attract the attention of other children who do not excel as well. Some of these children will seek help from such peers, but there will be some who might not like to see such associations. Hence, do be aware that there may be unforeseen repercussions from seemingly minute matters that should not bother anyone, but bother one or two people.

If the number you found was the number 8:

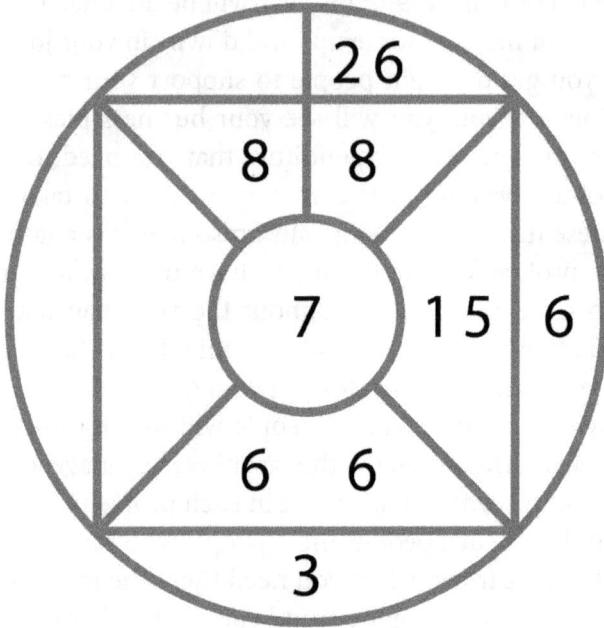

This year is a very interesting year for you. Indeed, you may find yourself in stressful and frustrating situations, always being so busy and hardly finding any time to relax! However, this year is also a good year for you to find supporters and the right people crucial to your success. Once you have found the right people to assist you, you can delegate tasks to them and free yourself of some time, you may however, need to spend some money on them to see the results. If you have already found these people before the year started, congrats! Your success and achievement will be more easily attainable. Do take note to ensure a work-life balance as being too busy with your career or business might cause some marriage tension that may lead to divorce. Do be aware that you may see large amount of money coming in and going out relatively fast.

For people born in 1901, 1910, 1919, 1928, 1937, 1946, 1955, 1964, 1973, 1982 and 1991, this year is particularly stressful for you so you have to really push yourself hard and to the limits. There are quite a few possible situations which can cause undue stress on you indeed. A couple of tips for you is to learn some good stress management techniques in order to de-stress, and to have a strong mind and body in preparation for the tasks ahead. You will be meeting a lot of new people but you should also be careful with the new network you are building as some of them may cause more harm than good, however unintentionally. This year, your career or business will require you to work and work, and you may find yourself spending more time and energy in it than before. You may also find yourself taking on some projects and doing them individually. You may have some family issues to settle if you keep working so hard and neglect your family, so you really have to ensure a good work-life balance and spend quality time with family and loved ones. In addition, there may be some legal matters that you need to settle as well. It is truly a trying year for you this year but as long as you can persevere through, you can see your just rewards!

For children born in 2009, they may find more temperamental this year due to a lot of stress and tension from the surroundings. These children may need to find someone who they can be comfortable with and talk to relieve their negative emotions and frustrations within. There is a possibility of increased workload this year and they need to be able to endure and persevere through this seemingly daunting task because hard work will pay off.

For people born in 1902, 1911, 1920, 1929, 1938, 1947, 1956, 1965, 1974, 1983 and 1992, this busy year can create a lot of stress and tension for you but it also means that you have a lot of work to do. There are opportunities for you to travel overseas for business but it is your choice whether you want to go or not. Your business should be fast and short-termed, like contract-based business or a lot of activity is involved, which is good for you, it keeps you on your toes. You may also find yourself doing tasks on your own, perhaps because of something you said. However, one thing to take note is not to let your frustrations get into you and cause you to speak unnecessarily. Hence, it is always good to keep work and personal matters separate and never let the frustrations cross over. Otherwise, you might find yourself speaking without thinking and causing a whole lot of unnecessary further issues. Most conflicts occurring this year is caused by a sharp tongue and hurtful words, so a gentle reminder to hold your tongue and think more before speaking. Remain calm and composed and things will work in your favour.

For children born in 2001 and 2010, you may find that these children have quite a bit of stress and frustration speaking, somehow people are not understanding what they are saying or their language is not clear. They cannot get their points across. Yet, they are meeting so many new friends and knowing so many people. It can be especially frustrating when meeting new friends for the first time and not getting clear communication between both of them. These children will be learning to be more independent this year. They may even be more proactive in their activities which is good!

For people born in 1903, 1912, 1921, 1930, 1939, 1948, 1957, 1966, 1975, 1984 and 1993, this year has a lot of stress and frustration coming from work and relationships. Work is getting more fast and unstable, with more ups and downs than normal, this causes you to feel a little unsure about the setting and quite pressurized at times too. It may also cause you to spend more than usual in an attempt to relieve stress, although you may experience a higher expenditure even without the pressure from work. This can create a financial burden. However, you may have opportunities to travel overseas for business, and this may cause some of you unnecessary stress while others may enjoy this. Some of you may have it worse as the possibility of leaving your job is there as well. Do also be aware that your heart is weak this year, and is prone to having issues this year, so please ensure a good nutrition plan and drink lots of water. Anyway, all the pressure may cause you to speak without thinking and at times, hurt other people unintentionally, especially in relationships. Hence, do consider learning some activity to relieve yourself of stress and help yourself in work and relationship matters. A fun and relaxing activity will help de-stress and may even help you to learn something about yourself. You have to endure this trying time in order to see your success and rewards!

For children born in 2002 and 2011, there is a lot of stress and frustration coming from studies and family. There may be some family issues that affect such children whether they want to let people know or not. These children may say hurtful things or show negative behaviours in an attempt not to tell others about what may be happening in the family. There is a possibility of a change of environment due to such incidents. Having such changes in the environment does allow these children to meet and make new friends, however, the cycle can repeat itself as long as the initial issue is not resolved. Such issues can also affect a child's studies.

For people born in 1904, 1913, 1922, 1931, 1940, 1949, 1958, 1967, 1976, 1985 and 1994, this year of stress comes mainly from relationships for you which is interesting indeed. Some of you may get married this year! And singles may have opportunities to meet that special someone. Indeed, this year has a lot of opportunities for you to meet people, but you have to be careful as there may be some not so good people amongst all the good people that you meet. It can be frustrating especially when two people barely know each other and try to do something together and yet meet obstacles in their plans or actions, hence, clear and concise communication is key. For people who are more business oriented, these people that you meet can be great network for future business, but again, do be aware of other people's intentions for why they want to work together. When dealing with your colleagues, clear instructions is also needed, otherwise, they may be susceptible to using unkind words under their own stress and pressure from work. You also need to be aware of what you say, as your own unkind words can be used against you as well. I know that it can be quite vexing when you are trying to handle everything but trust in those who can help you and things will get better. This year is truly an interesting year for you, isn't it?

For children born in 2003 and 2012, their studies and academics are doing well however, they may have family and relationships issues this year. And while these children have great potential to excel in academics, if they let the frustrations get to them, it can really affect their results. These children can meet a lot of new friends as well, but for those children born in 2003, they may mistake crushing on someone to be a good reason to get into a relationship, and this can be an issue when it does not go according to their plans. Teaching these children how to prioritise will be a good idea this year.

For people born in 1900, 1905, 1914, 1923, 1932, 1941, 1950, 1959, 1968, 1977, 1986 and 1995, this year has a lot of opportunities arising for good business. However, you need to establish a good work life balance as well, so that you can reduce the family and relationships issues that may arise. In a worst case scenario, there may be talk of divorce. Your work can be quite stressful and frustrating but you have to bear with it, because it will get quite fast and especially if you have a lot of activity involved or it is contract based job, it will be quite rewarding. In addition, you have a way with words and can motivate your colleagues when you need to. Getting such supporters on your side is also key to your success this year. With such strong support assisting you in your business, truly no one can stop you from achieving your just rewards this year!

For children born in 2004 and 2013, there may be some family issues that can create unnecessary stress and tension in these children. There is some possibility of a lot of movement between homes or schools and classrooms. Their work may seem unstable and inconsistent but ultimately, they can do reasonably well. These children need to learn how to open up to their problems and seek the right people for assistance when it gets to that.

For people born in 1906, 1915, 1924, 1933, 1942, 1951, 1960, 1969, 1978, 1987 and 1996, this is a year of high expenditure and financial difficulty for you and creates quite a bit of tension and stress with finances. However, persevering and taking calculated risks can help you to tide through and may even bring about an expected windfall! This year also provides you opportunities to present yourself and your ideas to people and make them truly believe in you. Gaining their support will help you in ways un-imagined, and truly no one can stop you from achieving your goals this year! All the challenges of this year will teach you many things, so learn from each experience and continue ahead!

For children born in 2000, 2005 and 2014, this year is a stressful year dealing with finances and emotions for these children. They have to learn how to present themselves to a greater audience as part of their curriculum. These children have to work very hard to push through the challenges that they may face this year.

For people born in 1907, 1916, 1925, 1934, 1943, 1952, 1961, 1970, 1979, 1988 and 1997, this year is an amazing year for you to achieve your desired outcomes and achieve your success! As long as you put your mind to it, you can achieve almost anything you want! Once you put your plans into action, you may find yourself meeting a lot of people, and truthfully, these people have the potential to be your supporters. With a strong group of supporters, you can assign specific tasks to them, ensuring that they are doing their best in what they do, and all these can help you greatly. You may at times feel stressed with dealing with people but it is all for a good cause, be positive when dealing with them and it will work out fine. Also remember to inform your supporters about the plans you have, so that everyone knows what is going on and how to achieve it together. Indeed, once everything falls into place, no one can stop you from achieving your goals!

For children born in 2006, these children have some issues when dealing with people. These issues arise because these children seem to have a duality in doing things, what this means is that they can be quite contrasting doing the same task; on one hand do this, on the other hand do that. This year, these children may be quite blunt and straightforward and unintentionally hurt their friends with their speech. Add that to the amount of new friends they are meeting and making and we have quite a few issues appearing.

For people born in 1908, 1917, 1926, 1935, 1944, 1953, 1962, 1971, 1980, 1989 and 1998, this year is a stressful and frustrating year for you, with occasional bouts of anger. Most of the issues seem to be with people, you can very stressed and frustrated dealing with people from seemingly everywhere, your colleagues, your clients, your friends, your family, strangers you meet on the street etc. A tip here is for you to maintain a healthy work life balance, as well as to separate work and family matters. You don't need to bring work issues into the family where it may create new family issues and that is taxing on anyone. Also, when dealing with your colleagues or clients, clear and concise communication is essential. This will help you in getting quality work back as well. You may also realize that it is how you present yourself, perhaps you present yourself in a manner that promotes negative feedback, and if so, present yourself in a genuine and positive manner to generate positive feedback. By the way, you may also experience high expenditure, but this also indicates great earnings, hence, control your expenditure and you should see quite a bit of income flowing in!

For children born in 2007, these children may experience quite a bit of family issues and disputes which can leave some of them very frustrated with themselves. If there are too many issues happening, these children may experience difficulty interacting with their peers as well, as what happens in at home has been transmitted to the social environment. All these frustrations can lead such children to be quite temperamental and emotional. If you know of such children, do provide some assistance and be there for them when they need someone to talk to.

For people born in 1909, 1918, 1927, 1936, 1945, 1954, 1963, 1972, 1981, 1990 and 1999, this year you will see that you have a higher expenditure than normal. You may also experience some ups and downs in your career and this can cause you a lot of stress and frustration. This can also cause you to continuously seek out opportunities to improve your career and business, and this can cause you to be rather busy with work. One of the areas you may consider is to go into investments, but do calculated risk management before going into it. Being so busy with work, you may find yourself having some family and relationship issues. Thus, it will be a good idea for you to have adequate work life balance, especially not to bring your frustrations from work into your family and personal life. Talk of divorce is the last thing you need. Being so busy at work, you are likely to meet new network potential as well as find the need to provide clear and concise instructions to your colleagues in order to assist you in work. Doing so will assist you at work and thus, improve the work quality, allowing you to achieve your desired returns in proper order.

For children born in 2008, these children are generally quiet and tend to keep things to themselves. This year, they may have family issues and disputes at home that cause them a lot of stress and frustrations. However, while they may seek people to be friends, they are not too comfortable with telling about their issues just yet. There is also academic stress which they have to deal with. All in all, if they can handle the stress and persevere, they are likely to develop a strong mind of their own, for their future success in life.

If the number you found was the number 9:

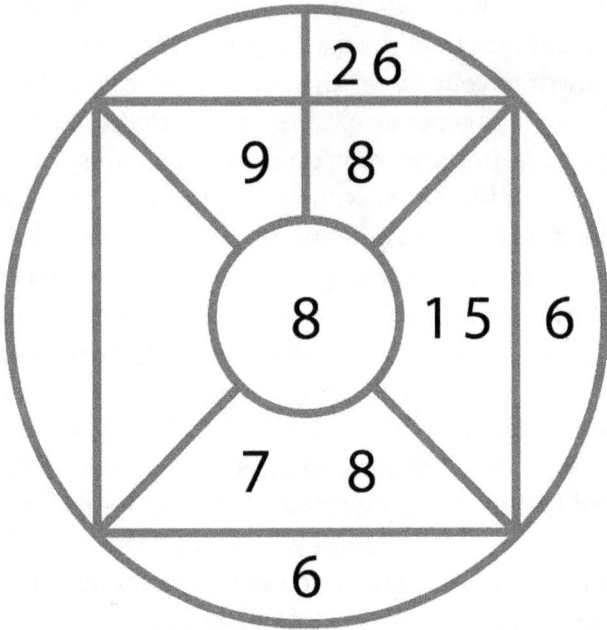

This year you are rather busy with work and business opportunities given to you by your network, and interestingly enough, you are still looking for more business opportunities! It can create quite a bit of stress and frustration but you know that hard work will pay off. Do ensure that you draw a clear line between work and family, for it may affect your marriage when work matters intrude into your family life. Know that dealing with people will create stress for you and you should persevere and delegate your job to see your returns. You have to be clear and concise in your communication, while managing your customers, your colleagues or even with your family. Plan your goals and not let anything stop you from your success!

For people born in 1901, 1910, 1919, 1928, 1937, 1946, 1955, 1964, 1973, 1982 and 1991, this year has some challenges that you have to face and overcome in order to achieve success. Among your network of supporters, there are some people who may not wish you success and may bring you more harm than good. In the worst case scenario, you may even become bankrupt. Hence, you should be aware of their true intentions before doing business together. Also, do remember to keep a line between work and family, and to keep it balanced between the two. Ensuring that you spend adequate time will reduce the possibility of family issues. You may feel frustrated at times but do hold your tongue especially if harsh words is on its tip. That can create more problems instead of solving anything. Think carefully before you speak, and that can help you to work wonders with people. Another thing to note this year is that you may be involved in an accident or in an operation, so do be aware for yourself and your loved ones. You may find yourself needing to plan in great detail about the goals that you have for yourself, as well as having to do and complete the subsequent tasks independently. Such independence and discipline can make you stress and seem like a workaholic. However, seek the right people to help you in the job, and you can rest your mind with these people at hand.

Now for children born in 2009, this year brings some challenges to these children. Their families may have issues and disputes which cause unnecessary stress on these children, with the possibility of these children taking it out on their friends with harsh words. These children need to find someone who they can talk to without holding back, someone they can trust and learn from at the same time. These children will learn to be more independent as well, learning to do thing by themselves and discovering the importance of knowing how to do it.

For people born in 1902, 1911, 1920, 1929, 1938, 1947, 1956, 1965, 1974, 1983 and 1992, this year will involve a lot of communication at work, and this can create quite a bit of stress on you. With the increase in meetings and presentations, it is little wonder you feel stressed and frustrated over it. Is necessary to communicate a lot this year. However, do be reminded not to let the stress and frustration get into your actual communication, otherwise, there may be hurtful words being spoken without meaning to. In addition, with so much communication going on, you are bound to meet many people and build a network, so it is prudent that you find the right people (such as ones having knowledge and technical skill) to mingle with and avoid the ones who gossip more. They say that loud vessels make the most noise. Finally, you can see greater success if you think before you talk, and choose your words wisely. Also, you have opportunities for go overseas for work-related purposes this year, although it is your choice whether you want to go or not.

For the children born in 2001 and 2010, there is an increase in the communication especially when showcasing their talents to their friends. These children are able to make a lot of new friends this year too. Some of them might be more daring and prone to taking risks so do keep an eye on them when possible. They should be careful of possible emotional outbursts and arguments between friends.

For people born in 1903, 1912, 1921, 1930, 1939, 1948, 1957, 1966, 1975, 1984 and 1993, this year brings about a lot of ups and downs in business and career for you, hence, your work will be rather fast-paced and unstable. You may even feel the urge to change job to something more stable and less pressurizing. You may also find yourself spending money easily and having higher than normal expenditure as a result of attempting to relieve stress. Do some financial budgeting and figure which expenses can be reduced in order to have more secure finances. There are some risky investments that you might encounter but do some calculated risk management and investment research before sinking into it, it can mean the difference between a huge loss and a huge gain. Also, when it concerns about your health, do take precaution! There is some concern for your liver and heart this year, so do get a medical check as soon as possible. There are also indicators of being involved in an accident or an operation as well!

For children born in 2002 and 2011, there is some stress and frustration this year for these children. Some of these children may experience family issues that upset them and cause them to have anger issues and possibly physical issues as well. They will then seek out new relationships for comfort and consolation. Generally these children are quite capable in their academics but if the stress is too much, they may have a dip in grades.

For people born in 1904, 1913, 1922, 1931, 1940, 1949, 1958, 1967, 1976, 1985 and 1994, there is a lot of planning involved this year for you. Some of you may find yourself planning a lot of things for your work while others find themselves planning for other people. Some of you may even find an increase in consulting for and offering advice to other people. Although you are knee-deep in planning, do remember that you need action to get the ball rolling as well. Over-planning can lead to more stress and frustration as well as other possible issues. Hence, plan just enough and get started with the tasks! Only then can we say truly, no one can stop you in your plans and endeavours! In addition, do be careful of being too rash in making friends and offering help, as some people may betray your trust instead. There is also some relationship and marriage issues that you may face or need to solve this year. Hence, do ensure a work-life balance and spend adequate quality time with your family and loved ones. Granted that you can be quite headstrong at times but do note that being flexible at the right time can work wonders especially where relationships are concerned.

For children born in 2003 and 2012, they have some stress and frustration when it comes to their studies. Generally, they can still cope with academics, however, their families may have issues as well. Such issues can affect their studies negatively so it will be ideal if there is someone who can assist them. However, such children can be very strong-willed and private children.

For people born in 1900, 1905, 1914, 1923, 1932, 1941, 1950, 1959, 1968, 1977, 1986 and 1995, this year is challenging for you and requires you to be focused in what you want to do this year. You may find yourself getting temperamental due to the challenges so you need to maintain your composure. Otherwise, it might get into your communication and affect your relationships with people. This can also lead you to attract some people who will do you more harm than good so do be aware. However, when you maintain your composure through such challenges, you can move people with your words and get them to do what you need them to do. In addition, there may be some opportunities for business overseas as well as many opportunities to meet rich and influential people. Such people can be great mentors and guide you through the challenges as well, allowing you to develop further. As mentioned earlier, this is a challenging year for you. You have to take precaution for your health and in the event of an accident. Avoid mountain climbing this year if possible. For a woman, there is some indication of pregnancy difficulty this year, hence, please work safely and take care of yourself.

For children born in 2004 and 2013, they have a challenging year ahead. This is a year where they need to learn a lot of things and overcome quite a few challenges by themselves. It will help them to develop into a better individual, provided they put their full efforts into it. This year, these children may experience some movement between locations, such as moving house and a change in school.

For people born in 1906, 1915, 1924, 1933, 1942, 1951, 1960, 1969, 1978, 1987 and 1996, this year is all about money! However, there is a lot of fast money, mainly from high expenditures and fast earnings. What this means is that you need to do some financial budgeting and consider stopping expenditure that is redundant. There is a chance for profits from investments this year, so do some risk calculation and seize the opportunity when it comes! However, you do need to ensure your health is in order. There is some indication of health issues affecting you this year, as well as an indication of an operation. In particular, you need to take note of your heart's condition as well as your kidneys and bladder, as they might be a bit weak. Some extra insurance would be great for you as well. All in all, although you need to keep your health in check, this is a great year for making a lot of profits!

For children born in 2000, 2005 and 2014, this can be an emotional year for these children. Especially for children in 2000 and 2005, who may need to learn some presentation skills and use them, this year can be a stressful year when it comes to work and academics too.

For people born in 1907, 1916, 1925, 1934, 1943, 1952, 1961, 1970, 1979, 1988 and 1997, this is a great year for networking and attaining your success! You will ensure that everything falls into place and that can kick-start your success. Your work will assist you in creating a lot of network and you have huge opportunities to meet rich and influential people and to find the right people to do the right tasks. However, when you meet so many people, there is a chance for you to meet some not so good people as well, and these people can sabotage your plans or backstab you, hence, do be aware of the intentions of the people you meet this year. Now singles have an opportunity to meet their potential partner this year, but for married people, please take note and beware. To sum up, act on your plans and success can be yours. Also, find the right mentor and learn as much as possible as well as find the right student to teach and develop. It will build your portfolio and help you to apply what you learn!

For children born in 2006, there is a lot of friendships to be made this year. These children may meet someone special this year as well, and crush on them easily. They need to learn the meaning of such emotions and not to fall too deeply. Some of these children may be a bit impulsive this year and speak without thinking, causing unnecessary issues later on. These children need to find a mentor to guide them and teach them the right knowledge.

For people born in 1908, 1917, 1926, 1935, 1944, 1953, 1962, 1971, 1980, 1989 and 1998, this year is a very stressful and frustrating year for you. There is a lot of anger and tension as well. This can create a heart issue for you this year, so do be aware. You may find yourself in so many busy situations that you may even feel lost or overwhelmed. You are busy preparing for presentations and yet, you have to deal with people from all over as well. Your boss and colleagues seem to give you a lot of stress but it is more frustrating dealing with people who don't seem to understand you. Truly, people management skills are key this year. Upon learning such skills and application of such skills, you will find yourself in a better position to handle workloads and tasks assigned by people. Another thing to note is to keep your work and personal life separated. There are tendencies where the stress and frustration from work gets into your personal life, and this can have an influence on your relationship with your family and loved ones. Learn to relax and de-stress and avoid having your stress unload on your significant other. There are indications of marriage and relationship issues this year which you may need to solve. Maintain a calm demeanour and think before you speak. Persevere such hardship and you will see rewards at the end!

For children born in 2007, there are some family issues that are occurring in their lives that may be escalating. These issues create unnecessary stress and tension in these children which affects their social and emotional development. It can affect their work too, but them having bursts of anger is not going to help. Helping the ones who have physical signs are easier, it is finding the silent ones who are not as easy to find and help.

For people born in 1909, 1918, 1927, 1936, 1945, 1954, 1963, 1972, 1981, 1990 and 1999, you may find your expenditure increasing this year, hence you may consider doing some financial planning and removing expenses that are no longer needed. Your work may have ups and downs and some instability partly because of last year's busy schedule and activities. If your career is already fast-paced or contract based, then this is a great year for you and your business. Otherwise, you might find the increase in activity may add additional pressure on you. There may be some risky investments that can yield profits, but a word of caution to approach such investments with a calculative mind. Ensure it is more profitable first before venturing.

For children born in 2008, these children are usually quite straight forward but may become more secretive this year. You may find them thinking and planning about things, as if they were contemplating something. They may have difficulty making friends in the beginning or have difficulty maintaining their friendships this year. It is alright if they need their own individual space and time until they get used to the new situation and environment.

www.ingramcontent.com/pod-product-compliance
Lightning Source LLC
Chambersburg PA
CBHW052137090426
42741CB00009B/2123